Travel and Tourism

Neil Punnett
Wilberforce Sixth Form College, Hull

Blackwell Education

Published by
Basil Blackwell Ltd
108 Cowley Road
Oxford OX4 1JF
England

British Library Cataloguing in Publication Data

Punnett, Neil
 Travel and tourism.
 1. Tourism
 I. Title
 338.4'791

 ISBN 0–631–90427–1 (school edition)
 ISBN 0–631–17667–5 (paperback)

Typeset in 11 on 12.5 point New Century Schoolbook
by Opus of Oxford
Illustrations by Trevor Mason
Printed in Hong Kong by Wing King Tong Co. Ltd

ACKNOWLEDGEMENTS

Government of Alberta 7, 39 (bottom); Alton Towers 11 (bottom left); Karen Anthony 48 (3); Beamish Museum 18 (left), 9 (top and bottom); Blackpool Tourist Board 9 (top); Centre Parcs 26 (3); Cephas 50 (right), 51 (left), 85 (left); James Davis Travel Photography 36 (top and bottom), 43 (bottom right); Patrick Doherty 21; Edinburgh Festival 43 (top left); French Railways 75 (top); Hoseasons Holidays 83 (1); Hulton–Deutsch 4; Italian Tourist Board 48 (top); Jorvik Viking Centre 71; Leatherhead Food Research Association 87; London Zoo 57 (1); Manchester Airport 5, 57 (1), 61 (top); His Grace the Duke of Marlborough 11 (top); Metrocentre 38 (top), 39 (top); NASA 34 (right); National Heritage 21 (top); National Railway Museum 9 (bottom); Christina Newman 10, 12, 13, 52, 77; QA Photolibrary 74 (bottom); Quality International 83 (1); Sealink (cover); Southend Tourist Board 17 (middle); Spanish Tourist Board 14 (right), 30, 46, 47; Spectrum 35; Katy Squire 57 (2), 60 (top and bottom), 66; Louise Stewart/ Richard Spilsbury 51 (right), 67; Swiss Tourist Board 11 (bottom right), 32, 33; Lynn Tait 17 (right); Thomson Holidays 12 (top), 14 (left), 28, 31; Graham Topping 9 (left and right), 23 (left), 43 (top right), 57 (5), 61 (bottom), 70, 83 (1), 90; Turkish Tourist Office 50 (left), 85 (right); TWA 72, 73; Welsh Tourist Board 43 (bottom left); York Tourist Board 44 (left and right), 45 (top); Yorkshire Dales National Park 22, 23 (right).

CONTENTS

INTRODUCTION

1 THE HISTORICAL DEVELOPMENT OF TOURISM IN EUROPE

The word 'travel' comes from the French word *travail*, which means 'work'. The word 'tourism' also comes from a French word – *autour*, which means 'around'.

Before the building of good roads and railways in the early 19th century, travel really was hard work!

How long would it take you to travel by coach from London to Edinburgh? 12 hours? 15? 200 years ago it would have taken you ten days! Your 'coach' would have been horse-drawn, and you would have bumped over rutted cart tracks, not smooth motorways. Few people attempted to travel long distances. Travellers were mostly soldiers, traders, explorers and religious pilgrims. In some countries, people were not allowed to travel away from their home area.

Tourism

Since travelling was so difficult and uncomfortable, it's hardly surprising that few people travelled for pleasure. Tourism is a relatively recent development. Fig A suggests why:

Tourism needs:

1 **Leisure time – but**

- 200 years ago few people had 'holidays' as we know them. The only days of rest were religious 'holy days' such as Christmas and Easter.
- there were no paid holidays. Most people did not earn enough money to take time off work.

2 **Money – but**

- transport was expensive. Most people could not afford to pay for the journey, or stop work for the time it would take.

3 **Speed and comfort – but**

- bad roads and primitive methods of transport made travelling uncomfortable and even dangerous.
- there were no bicycles, cars, railways, aircraft or steam ships.
- travel arrangements were complicated – there were no telephones, computers or credit cards.

Fig. A

The first tourists were wealthy people. In the early 17th century members of some European royal families began to travel to towns where there were springs of water containing special minerals. They believed that drinking and bathing in the water was good for their health. (The Romans had developed this idea centuries before – you can still see the Roman Baths at Bath, in Avon.)

Other wealthy people soon followed the royal lead. Spa towns such as Bath and Harrogate in England, Spa in Belgium and Baden-Baden in Germany became centres for fashionable society.

Fig. B   Aristocrats on the Grand Tour

In the late 18th century seawater was recommended as a health cure. Royalty and wealthy people travelled to resorts such as Brighton and Scarborough to bathe in the sea – and even drink the water. English aristocrats also travelled further afield. A 'Grand Tour' of European cities such as Paris, Florence and Venice (centres of art and culture) was a 'must' for every educated aristocrat (Fig B).

Thomas Cook

Foreign travel was still far beyond the means of most middle- or working-class people. But in the 19th century the ideas of one man sowed the seeds of modern mass tourism (tourism for all). His name was Thomas Cook.

In 1841 Cook persuaded the Midland Counties Railway Company to run a special train from Leicester to Loughborough, for a temperance meeting. (Look up the meaning of "temperance" in a dictionary.) This was probably the first publicly-advertised excursion train in England. Cook organised many more excursions within England. Then, in 1855, he began to take groups of people from Leicester to the French town of Calais.

The next year, Cook led a long-distance tourist excursion through Europe. He advertised it as "Cook's Grand Tour". The trip was similar to today's package tours. He offered people transport, accommodation, meals and sightseeing tours at a single, all-inclusive price. These tours gave middle-class people in Britain the chance of foreign travel.

In the early 1860s Cook stopped leading the tours himself. He became an agent for the sale of domestic and overseas travel tickets. His company was the first travel agency – and it is still one of Britain's largest travel agents. More and more people wanted to travel abroad. More travel agencies were set up to cater for them.

Travel for all

In the early 20th century more ordinary working people were given paid holidays. This meant that they could afford to go away for a day or two, or perhaps a week, often to popular seaside resorts like Southend or Blackpool. Foreign travel, though, was still far too expensive for ordinary people.

During the Second World War (1939–45) thousands of British men and women travelled abroad as members of the Allied forces. Many acquired a taste for foreign travel.

People in the developed world became, in general, much richer during the 1950s and 60s. They enjoyed a higher standard of living than ever before and had longer, paid holidays. Advances in technology meant that travel was faster and more comfortable. The holiday industry boomed. Companies competed to offer cheap package deals to Mediterranean resorts (Fig C).

In 1950 25 million foreign holidays were taken worldwide. By 1989 this number had leapt to 330 million. Tourism is now the world's second largest industry.

QUESTIONS

1 What do the origins of the word 'travel' tell you about the problems facing early travellers?
2 (a) What is a spa?
  (b) Name three spas in the UK.
  (c) Why were spas important to the development of tourism?
3 What was the 'Grand Tour'? Who went on it?
4 What is a package tour? Explain the role of Thomas Cook in the development of mass tourism.
5 Study Figs B and C.
  (a) List the similarities and differences between these two types of tourism.
  (b) Compare your list with a partner. Discuss the two lists and agree what to include in a final list.

Fig. C   Holidaymakers disembark from a charter airline at a Spanish resort

5

2 THE GROWTH OF LEISURE TIME

In recent years, most people in the UK have enjoyed increasing amounts of leisure time. Fig A shows how the number of hours in the average working week in the UK has gone down since 1960. The resulting extra hours of non-working time are available for leisure. From Fig B you can see how the length of paid holidays in the UK has increased since 1960 – when the average was 10 days per year – to 1989, when the average was 23 days.

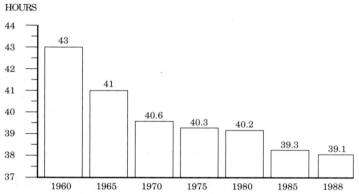

HOURS

Fig. A   Average working week for full-time employees in the UK (excluding overtime)

Together, these two social changes have had a dramatic effect on the growth of the tourist and leisure industry. Shorter working weeks plus longer paid holidays mean more leisure time. Add this to the rapid increase in disposable income (that is, the money available to spend once all necessities and bills have been paid for) and the result is a greatly increased demand for tourist and leisure facilities.

The number of people taking a second, or a third, holiday each year has increased. In 1960, only 6% of people in the UK had more than one holiday each year. By 1989, 24% were taking more than one holiday. In 1960, 46% of people had no holiday at all. By 1989 this figure had fallen to 36%. Fig C shows the numbers of holidays taken by UK residents, and where they were taken.

	1966	1971	1976	1981	1987
In UK	31	34	38	37	37
Abroad	5	7	8	13	20
Total	36	41	46	50	57
UK Population	54.7	55.61	55.89	56.45	56.68

Fig. C   Holidays taken by residents of the UK (millions)

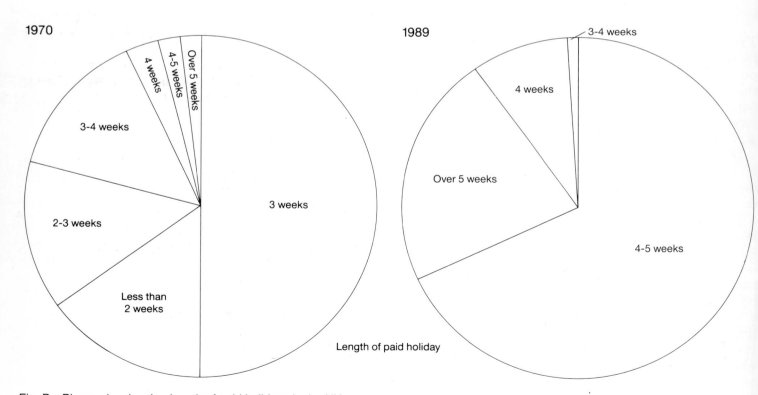

Fig. B   Pie graphs showing length of paid holidays in the UK

Other factors have influenced the tourist industry:

1 The increase in car ownership has meant that people go on more day trips, more short breaks and more domestic holidays, with little need for forward planning.

2 People are becoming more aware of the importance of leisure for health – everyone needs a break from the routine of life.

Fig. D   Modern leisure centres offer a wide range of sport and leisure facilities

3 A greater choice of holidays and leisure facilities is now available; these generate increased demand (ie newer, better facilities make more people want to use them). For example, leisure centres like Fig D have opened in most major towns. This has encouraged more people to participate in a range of sports and leisure activities.

Tourism and its related industries are now one of the UK's major employers. Money spent by visitors from abroad contributes to the UK economy – tourism is an important source of foreign exchange (Fig E).

QUESTIONS

1 Copy and complete the table below:

Increasing leisure time in the UK

Trend	Change			
Longer holidays	1960:	10 days per year	1989: ?	days per year
Shorter working week	1960:	? hours	1989: ?	hours
People taking holidays	1960:	54 %	1989: ?	%
More than one holiday	1960:	? %	1989: ?	%

2 In 1960 there were 8 million cars in the UK; by 1990 there were 18 million. How has this increase in car ownership affected tourism and leisure in the UK?

3 How is tourism important to Britain (Fig E)?

4 (a) Draw a line graph to show the statistics in Fig C.

(b) What percentage of total holidays were taken abroad in (i) 1971 and (ii) 1987? What factors may account for the change?

The importance of the tourist industry in the UK

* 1.5 million people are employed.

* 50 000 new jobs are created each year.

* Tourism is the UK's fastest growing industry.

* Within England alone UK residents spent £5600 million in 1986.

* 15.6 million overseas visitors to the UK spent over £6700 million in 1987.

* Only the USA, Spain, Italy and France earn more from tourism than the UK.

Fig. E   The importance of the tourist industry in the UK

3 REASONS FOR TRAVEL AND A CLASSIFICATION OF DESTINATIONS

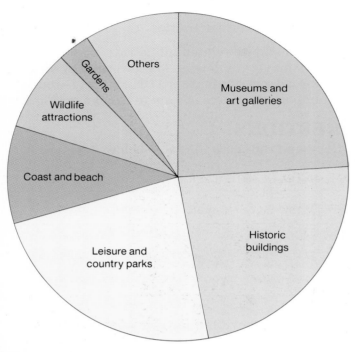

Fig. A   Visitors to English tourist attractions

Why do people travel for leisure? Fig A shows the percentage breakdown of visitors to English tourist attractions. This covers over 200 million visits, including those made by foreign visitors. Museums, galleries and historic buildings account for almost half the visitors: Britain's history and culture are vitally important to the tourist industry.

Fig B is based on a recent survey by the Countryside Commission. They asked a random sample of town-dwellers to fill in a questionnaire about their reasons for visiting the countryside.

QUESTIONS

1 Study Fig A. What percentage of visitors go to the following types of attraction:
   (a) Museums and art galleries?
   (b) Coast and beach?
   (c) Historic buildings?
2 Study Fig B. What percentage of trips to the countryside are:
   (a) Drives and picnics?
   (b) Visits to country parks?
   (c) Visits to the coast or beach?

Fig. B   Reasons for trips to the countryside

1	Blackpool Pleasure Beach	(10.2 million)
2	The British Museum, London	(3.6 million)
3	The National Gallery, London	(3.1 million)
4	St Paul's Cathedral, London	(3.0 million)
5	The Science Museum, London	(2.8 million)
6	Westminster Abbey, London	(2.7 million)
7	The Natural History Museum, London	(2.5 million)
8	Madam Tussaud's, London	(2.4 million)
9	Alton Towers, Staffordshire	(2.3 million)
10	The Tower of London	(2.2 million)
11	Albert Dock, Liverpool	(2.2 million)
12	York Minster	(2.2 million)
13	Canterbury Cathedral	(2.1 million)
14	Victoria and Albert Museum, London	(2.1 million)
15	Windsor Castle	(1.5 million)
16	The Tate Gallery, London	(1.4 million)
17	London Zoo	(1.3 million)
18	National Maritime Museum, London	(1.2 million)
19	National Railway Museum, York	(1.1 million)
20	Thorpe Park, Surrey	(1.1 million)

Fig. C   Britain's top 20 tourist attractions. (Numbers of visitors are given in brackets)

3 Figure C shows Britain's top 20 tourist attractions in order of the number of visitors they receive a year.
(Note, the list doesn't include 'natural' attractions like countryside/seaside.)
(a) In pairs, study the table and divide the list into types of attractions, eg seaside resort, theme park etc.

(b) Locate the 20 sites on an outline map of the UK by giving each its number. Add a key to the places.
(c) Can you see any pattern(s) in the distribution of the tourist attractions? Try to explain the patterns.

4 Fig D shows four well-known tourist locations in the UK. Which of these attractions would you most like to visit, and why?

(i) Blackpool

(ii) The Tower of London ▽

(iii) St Paul's Cathedral, London ▽

(iv) National Railway Museum, York ◁

Fig.D   Tourist locations in the UK

4 TOURIST DESTINATIONS

This unit looks at a number of different tourist environments. Study the photographs, then answer the questions below.

QUESTIONS

1 Briefly describe the scene in each of the photographs (Fig A – Fig F).
2 Copy and complete the table below:

	A	B	C	D	E	F
Type of tourist destination						
Why tourism has flourished there						
Possible tourist activities						
Typical person attracted, and where they might come from						

3 Form groups of three or four. Exchange your tables and discuss them. Then draw up a single table which represents the group's collective opinion.
4 In your group, discuss how you think the tourist developments at each of the places might have affected the environment.
(a) What are the benefits?
(b) What are the disadvantages?
(c) How could the facilities be improved?
5 As individuals, choose the three places you would most like to visit and arrange them in your order of preference. Take turns to explain your choice to the rest of the group.

Fig. A   Lake Windermere

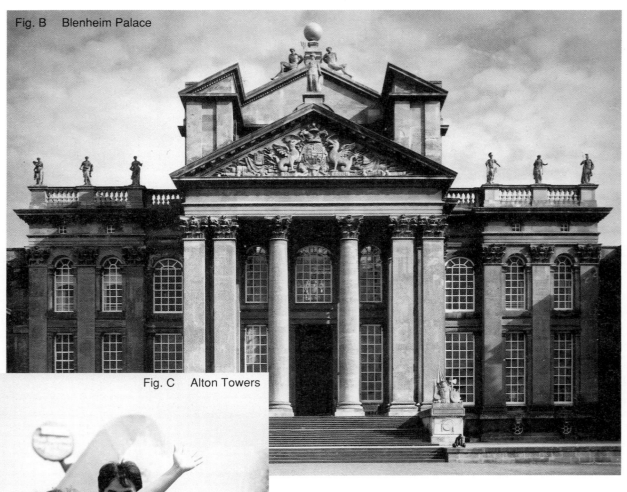
Fig. B   Blenheim Palace

Fig. C   Alton Towers

Fig. D   Zermatt

Fig. E   Benidorm ▲

▼ Fig. F   Bangkok, Thailand

5 FACTORS WHICH AFFECT THE CHOICE OF TOURIST DESTINATIONS

Fig. A   Travel companies compete to attract most holidaymakers

Why do some areas attract more tourists than others? A variety of factors may affect the tourist's choice. Some of them are:

1 **Cost**   This is an important factor, but it is not a simple case of 'the cheaper the better'. Some tourists seek out the cheapest holidays they can find, others are more concerned about value for money. Many are prepared to pay more to be sure of good facilities and good service.

Competition between different travel companies (Fig A) means that they may offer identical holidays at different prices. This forms an important part of some firms' advertising campaigns. Economies of scale operate in the travel industry, just as in any other: a large company which arranges holidays for many thousands of tourists (ie has high purchasing power) can strike better deals with hoteliers and airlines than a smaller company. The large company can pass on some of these price cuts to the customer – which, in turn, means that more people will want to travel with that company.

2 **Site facilities**   Resorts which can offer a wide variety of facilities are likely to attract more tourists. Opportunities for sport and recreation are particularly valuable. Many tourists (especially the young) expect a busy and varied nightlife, and seek resorts which have bars, clubs, discos etc (Fig B). However, increasing numbers of tourists try to *avoid* resorts

13

with too many facilities. They prefer a simpler, quieter holiday in a less commercialised resort (Fig C).

3 Availability Travel companies are most likely to invest in areas where they are welcome, where they can make the most profit, and where there is a proven market (ie they know people want to go there).

4 Safety It is important that people feel safe when they are on holiday. News reports of violence and lawlessness in a country will dissuade many people from taking holidays there (Fig D). The threat of terrorism can have the same effect. There was a dramatic drop in the numbers of American tourists visiting Europe in 1986, due to fears of reprisals after a US air raid on Libya.

5 Distance Many people want to reach their holiday destination as quickly as possible. This is the concept of *time-distance*. For example, Greek islands with their own airports attract many more visitors than neighbouring islands which can only be reached by ferry. For some people, however, travelling a great distance is part of the attraction of the holiday. Far Eastern destinations became popular during the 1980s, especially with people who found the Mediterranean resorts too congested. Nevertheless, nearly all tourists want their travel to be as easy as possible: this is sometimes termed *convenience-distance*.

6 Diffusion People are attracted to an area when they hear good reports in the media, or recommendations from friends who have holidayed there. In this way, the attractions of a tourist destination diffuse, or are spread, through an ever-wider number of people. New areas become fashionable. In the late 1970s the Greek Islands were *the* trendy holiday destination. In the mid-1980s Turkey was the place to be seen.

Fig. B A busy street in Benidorm

Fig. C A quiet, almost deserted Spanish village

QUESTIONS

1 Give three ways in which cost may affect choice of holiday.
2 Study Figs B and C.
  (a) List the type of facilities available at each place. How do they differ?
  (b) Suggest what sort of tourist would prefer a holiday at each destination, and why.
3 Why would few travel companies be likely to invest in:
  (a) Northern Ireland?
  (b) Libya?
4 How can distance affect a tourist's choice of holiday destination?
5 In groups, discuss the following questions:
  (a) What are the most fashionable holiday destinations today?
  (b) What factors make a holiday destination become fashionable or lose popularity?
  (c) Where did each group member last take a holiday? What factors affected the choice?
  (d) Fig E shows one student's attempt to work out a flow diagram covering all the factors that affect choice of holiday destination. Discuss the diagram in your group and try to develop an improved version, covering more factors.

Fig. D   Bad news for tourism

WHAT DO I WANT FROM MY HOLIDAY? — Sun and beach

⬇

WHERE CAN I GET THIS? — Greece, Spain, Seychelles, Kenya, Florida, Australia

⬇

HOW MUCH CAN I AFFORD? — £450

⬇

HOW LONG CAN I TAKE? — 10 days

⬇

WHERE CAN I GO FOR £450 FOR 10 DAYS? — Greece, Spain, Florida

Fig. E   What affects a tourist's choice of holiday destination?

6 CASE STUDY ONE: A SEASIDE RESORT

Around the British Isles there are hundreds of seaside resorts. Fig A shows the 20 most popular resorts in England and Wales. Many of these towns have similar histories. This unit looks at Southend-on-Sea in Essex, one of the largest resorts.

Fig B describes the development of Southend, from a tiny fishing settlement to a modern seaside resort.

Nowadays, people expect more from a resort than a promenade, a pier and amusement arcades. A few resorts have invested millions of pounds in major tourist facilities. At Bridlington, in Humberside, a vast indoor complex called Leisure World has been built. This holds three separate swimming pools, a solarium, a sauna, a multi-sports hall, a 100-seat theatre, five bars and restaurants, all under one roof. Is this is the answer for Southend?

Fig. A   The top 20 seaside resorts in England and Wales

18th century	Area now occupied by Southend-on-Sea was a quiet, empty stretch of coast. There was a tiny fishing village named South End.
1801	Princess Charlotte stayed at South End. She bathed and walked along the low cliffs. Her visit helped to make South End a popular resort with the wealthy. People could travel along the turnpike road from London or down the River Thames.
Early 19th century	Hotels and boarding houses were built. The village grew into a small town which called itself Southend-on-Sea. By 1841 it had a population of 5000.
1856	Railway from London reached Southend. This encouraged further slow population growth: Southend was London's nearest resort.
1889	A second railway was opened from London to Southend. As the standard of living of working people rose and the number of paid holidays increased, the people of London's East End were able to visit Southend on day trips. The longest pleasure pier in the world was built out into the Thames Estuary. More jobs were created and the population of Southend grew rapidly.
1911	Southend's population tripled within ten years! This was the golden age for Britain's seaside resorts.
1920s – 1950s	Southend continued to grow very rapidly, sprawling across many km of farmland. There were now over 10 km of seafront promenade with a 'Golden Mile' of amusement arcades, fun fairs and stalls selling shellfish and souvenirs. By 1930 the population had reached 115, 000. New types of people were moving to Southend. Commuters travelled to work in London each day by train, but chose to live in the pleasant surroundings of Southend. Retired people moved to Southend to seek peace and quiet and to enjoy the seaside and the mild climate. Southend began to diversify its economy away from tourism. Its own industries began to develop.
Late 1960s	The number of holidaymakers visiting Southend began to fall because of competition from cheap overseas holidays. Ironically many people came to Southend to fly from its airport to the Mediterranean sunspots.
1970s	Southend's seafront looked poor and decrepit. There was little investment in new facilities. The famous pier was badly damaged by fire and not repaired. The town turned its back on the sea and concentrated on its new jobs boom: offices. Many companies and government organisations moved from London to Southend, including Access credit cards, the VAT centre and HM Customs and Excise.
1980s	In recent years there has been increased investment in the seafront facilities. The pier has been rebuilt. There have been a number of special events including an annual airshow above the beach. However, the town's emphasis appears to be on making the most of the seafront for its own population, a recognition that tourism will form only a minor part of the town's economy in the future.

Fig. B   Southend through time

Fig. C

Fig. D (i)   Southend in the 1950s

Fig. D (ii) Modern Southend

The population of Southend-on-Sea between 1811 and 1981																		
Year	1811	1821	1831	1841	1851	1861	1871	1881	1891	1901	1911	1921	1931	1941	1951	1961	1971	1981
Population (thousands)	2	3	4	5	7	9	10	12	15	20	61	92	115	132	148	165	163	157

The climate of Southend-on-Sea												
Month	J	F	M	A	M	J	J	A	S	O	N	D
Temperature (°C)	4	5	7	9	12	16	18	18	16	12	8	4
Sunshine hours per day	1.7	2.6	4.2	5.5	7	7.5	7	6.6	5.2	3.7	2	1.5
Rainfall (mm)	48	36	33	41	41	33	51	50	40	56	61	48

Annual average rainfall: 538 mm; temperature range: 14°C; Daily average sunshine hours: 4.6

Fig. E   Southend-on-Sea: population and climate

QUESTIONS

1 Where is Southend-on-Sea?

2 Study Figs B and C. What advantages did the site of Southend-on-Sea have as a seaside resort?

3 Compare the two views in Fig D. How has Southend changed since the first photographs was taken? What aspects remain the same?

4 Study Fig E.
 (a) Draw a line graph to show the population of Southend between 1811 and 1981.
 (b) Add the following labels to your line graph, by way of explanation:
  second railway from London; small resort for the wealthy; commuters and retired people move to Southend; decline of resort; booming resort for day-trippers; first railway from London.

5 Study Fig E.
 (a) Draw a second graph to illustrate the temperature and rainfall statistics. Use bars for the rainfall and a line for the temperature.
 (b) Name the two warmest months.
 (c) Name the two driest months.
 (d) Name the two sunniest months.
 (e) Which month do you think would be best for a holiday in Southend? Give reasons for your choice.

6 (a) Why have British seaside resorts declined in popularity for holidays?
 (b) What would you do to increase their popularity?

7 Design a brochure to advertise the attractions of Southend-on-Sea as a holiday resort today. You want to persuade families to go there instead of to another British resort, or overseas. Think about travel costs as well as what Southend has to offer as a resort.

7 CASE STUDY TWO: A HERITAGE MUSEUM – BEAMISH

Fig A shows a scene in a North-Eastern town about 100 years ago. All is not what it seems, however. This is the Beamish North of England Open Air Museum. The people are actors in period costume. The buildings are genuine enough, but they were moved here, brick-by-brick, from towns and villages throughout the county of Durham. The railway station, for instance (Fig D), was brought from Rowley. Fig B shows the layout of Beamish.

Fig. A Staff outside the Beamish Co-operative stores

Beamish is a new kind of tourist attraction. It aims to re-create both industrial and farming life using genuine historic machinery and buildings. It is a kind of living museum which gives visitors the opportunity to experience at first hand what it was like to live and work in County Durham in the past. Visitors can put on hard hats and accompany a former miner underground at the reconstructed colliery (Fig C). As you walk down the dark, narrow, cold, dripping tunnel to the coalface it is easy to imagine the difficult and unpleasant conditions in which the miners worked.

Crafts such as mat making, horse-shoeing and baking bread are demonstrated in the Museum buildings. The costumed actors are also guides. They talk to the visitors about life 100 years ago and point out particular items of interest.

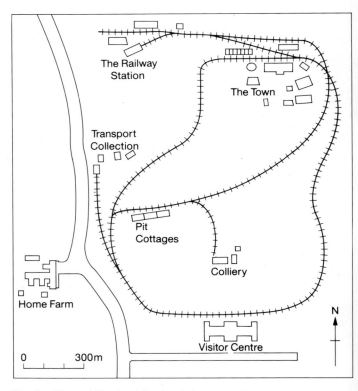

Fig. B Plan of North of England Open Air Museum

Home Farm is one of the few buildings which was originally built on its current site. Once visitors have negotiated the noisy flock of geese and entered the farmyard, they can see many old farm implements. Pride of the collection is a gleaming steam tractor which is still in working order. Steam tractors replaced farm horses; Home Farm includes a section devoted to these horses and their decorated harnesses.

The museum site covers 80 hectares. Visitors can travel from one area to another by tram or by steam train. If they alight at Rowley Station they will find it almost exactly as it was in 1876 (Fig D). At the station there is a massive locomotive built by the pioneer railway engineer George Stephenson in 1822.

The Open Air Museum was opened in 1971 on a site that was originally part of the Beamish Hall Estate. Since then it has expanded and has become one of the most popular tourist attractions in the North East of England. Several other open air museums have been opened, in different parts of the country. They include the Black Country Museum at Dudley and the Ironbridge Gorge Museum in Shropshire.

QUESTIONS
1 Describe the scenes in the three photographs.
2 (a) What are the special attractions of the North of England Open Air Museum?
  (b) Why do people want to visit such a museum?
3 Why was Beamish a good location for such a museum?
4 Design a poster advertising the North of England Open Air Museum.

Fig. C   Colliery at Beamish

Fig. D   Rowley Railway Station at Beamish

8 CASE STUDY THREE: AN HISTORIC SITE – STONEHENGE

Stonehenge has stood on Salisbury Plain for over 4000 years (Fig A). This mysterious stone circle, set on the remote, windswept plain, has fascinated and intrigued visitors for centuries. Who built it? How were the stones (weighing up to 45 tonnes each) carried to the site? What was its purpose – a temple? an astronomical observatory? a ceremonial meeting place?

The first written record of Stonehenge dates from the 12th century. Today, the site attracts over half a million visitors a year, making it one of Britain's important tourist attractions. But Stonehenge faces problems – some of them caused simply by the numbers of visitors to the site.

1 The grass has been eroded by the trampling of millions of feet. Steel mesh paths have now been laid and there are notices warning people to keep to the paths.

2 On a number of occasions vandals attacked the stones and sprayed graffitti. The circle has been fenced off and visitors can no longer walk among the stones.

3 Facilities had to be built to cope with the numbers of cars and coaches coming to the site. A large car park has been built across the road from Stonehenge. It is linked to the stone circle by a pedestrian subway.

4 The busy A344 and A303 roads pass close by Stonehenge. The traffic causes noise and pollution, destroying the mysterious atmosphere of the stone circle.

Fig B shows Stonehenge in the 1970s; Fig C shows Stonehenge today. The facilities provided for tourists (car parks, admission turnstiles, an exhibition room) have changed the character of Stonehenge. Many people protest about the intrusive paths, notices and fences. Yet it is clear that Stonehenge must be protected so that visitors can go on enjoying it. One suggested solution to this problem has been to build a replica of Stonehenge on a nearby site, in order to protect the original!

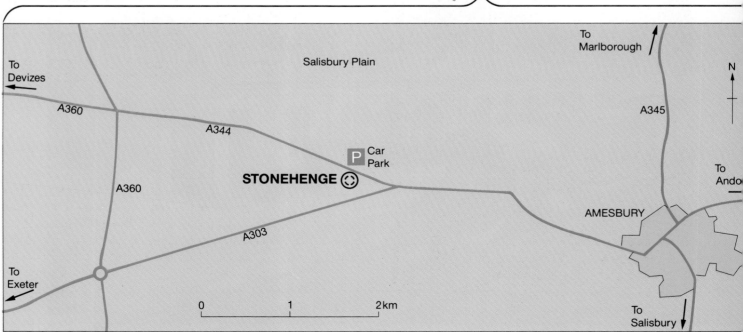

Fig. A   Site of Stonehenge

Fig. B   Stonehenge 1977

Fig. C   Stonehenge today

QUESTIONS

1 Where is Stonehenge?
2 What are the attractions of Stonehenge to tourists?
3 Study Figs B and C
  (a) Describe the scenes in the two photographs.
  (b) What evidence is there of measures taken to control visitors?
  (c) Which scene would you prefer to see if you were visiting Stonehenge?
4 Consider each of the measures taken at Stonehenge. For each, state why it has been taken and whether you agree with it:
  (a) Steel mesh footpaths.
  (b) Fences.
  (c) Car park.
  (d) Subway.
5 Form groups of three or four. Your task is to prepare a plan for Stonehenge which will give visitors maximum access to the stone circle but still protect it. Discuss the different approaches you could choose and agree on a plan. Produce notes and diagrams to support your plan. Present your plan to the rest of the class, allowing time for discussion of the advantages and disadvantages of your plan.

9 CASE STUDY FOUR: THE YORKSHIRE DALES

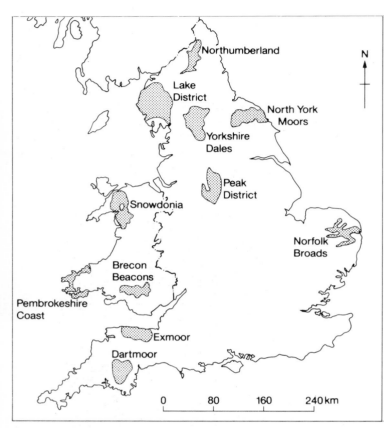

Fig. A   National Parks of England and Wales

The map shows the location of Britain's National Parks. There are 11 of them. Each has its own unique character and appeal, but it is possible to classify them as follows:

Mountainous highland areas Lake District, Snowdonia, Yorkshire Dales, Brecon Beacons
High moorland areas Peak District, Dartmoor, Northumberland
Lower moorland areas Exmoor, North York Moors
Coastal and water Pembrokeshire Coast, Norfolk Broads

National Parks were established following the National Parks and Access to the Countryside Act of 1949. Parliament only passed this Act after a lot of hard work by several groups of people, such as the Ramblers' Association and the Campaign for the Protection of Rural England, who were keen to preserve the countryside.

The National Parks occupy about 10% of the area of England and Wales. Each National Park is administered by a Park Authority. Its duties are:

(i) to preserve and enhance the natural landscape;
(ii) to promote the enjoyment of the National Parks by the public.

The establishment of a National Park does not affect the land ownership. Less than 2% of the land area of the Parks belongs to the Park Authorities. About 75% of the land is privately owned. The remaining 23% is owned by government organisations such as the Ministry of Defence or the Forestry Commission.

The Park Authority does not have an easy job. It has to try to reconcile the needs of tourists and local people. These needs or interests often conflict. For example, local people may support the construction of a new road to improve access to the area, or the establishment of a new factory to provide jobs. The Park Authority may have to try to prevent this because of the effects upon the landscape, which would reduce the area's appeal to tourists.

When the Parks were first established it was assumed that farmers and landowners would preserve the landscape very much as it had been before the Second World War. However, intensive farming methods have changed the British landscape dramatically – and this includes the National Parks. The increasing popularity of the National Parks has also caused problems. Better roads and increased car ownership mean that more and more tourists visit the National Parks. Traffic congestion is so bad that cars are banned from some 'problem areas' on summer weekends.

Fig B shows a typical view in the Yorkshire Dales. This unique and beautiful area is part of the Pennine Hills. Most of the land is over 180 metres high and there are several summits over 600 metres. Streams rise on the high fells and descend through rocky gorges with dramatic waterfalls, to join rivers in the steep-sided dales.

The Yorkshire Dales National Park was established in 1954. It covers an area of 1761 square kilometres (Fig C). 18 500 people live within the park area. Their grey stone farms and villages blend with the surrounding landscape. Carboniferous limestone rock has produced most of the dramatic scenery of the Dales. There are spectacular areas of bare limestone called pavements; beneath the surface there are complex networks of caves and caverns.

The National Park Committee does not own much land, but it encourages appropriate management of the landscape through the methods shown in Fig D. Over eight million people visit the Park each year. Six information centres cater for some of their needs.

Fig. B Ingleborough, in the Yorkshire Dales

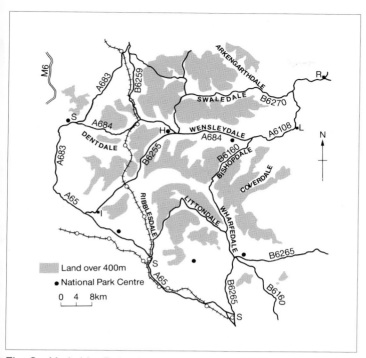

Fig. C   Yorkshire Dales National Park

complained that large areas of grazing land were being destroyed.

What could be done? One option considered was to close the area to walkers for five years to allow the soil to recover. This was dismissed as impractical. Instead, in April 1987 the National Park Committee launched the Three Peaks Project to repair the paths. Stone-based footpaths are being laid by machine. The result is a track rather than a path, which can be seen over a considerable distance. Once the tracks are laid, the land on either side can be restored. Over a few years the new track will weather and merge in with its surroundings. The Three Peaks Project is funded by the Parks Committee, the Countryside Commission and the Nature Conservancy Council: the total cost will be over £600 000.

Fig. E   Footpath erosion is a serious problem in some parts of the Dales

Each centre has an informative display, and books and maps are on sale. National Park staff are available to meet and advise the public, lead guided walks and lecture to groups.

Unfortunately, tourism brings problems to the National Park. Cars create noise and fumes, careless visitors leave litter and cause damage. The sheer volume of visitors is itself a problem: some of the most popular areas are being eroded by countless feet (Fig E). A footpath survey in 1986 revealed that of the 65 kilometres of paths in the Three Peaks area, one-third were severely damaged and in need of immediate repair. A further 21 km were in danger. As the footpath turned into a quagmire, walkers had spread out and trampled down the pathside vegetation. Their search for a mud-free route had created paths with an average width over twice that of a road! This created ugly scars on the landscape, and farmers

---

The National Park Committee manages the Dales landscape by:
- using the planning controls on development which acts of parliament give to all local authorities;
- offering free advice for those who plan to alter the landscape, such as farmers planning extensions to their buildings;
- making agreements with landowners and farmers for access to countryside or for management of landscape in traditional ways, such as retaining the drystone walls;
- improving the landscape, where possible, by tree planting, removal of eyesores and restoring architecturally or historically important buildings;
- repairing damage caused by improper use of the countryside, such as clearing litter.

Fig. D   How the National Park Commitee manages the landscape of the Dales

QUESTIONS

1 In a recent survey most people questioned thought that: (a) National Parks are owned by the Government; and (b) their sole aim is to meet the needs of tourists.
   Were they right? If not, why not (see Fig A)?
2 (a) How are farming and increasing popularity putting pressure on the National Parks?
   (b) Suggest ways of coping with this pressure.
3 Copy Fig C. Use an atlas to help you name the major towns on the map.
4 What are the attractions of the Yorkshire Dales for tourists?
5 How does the National Park Committee manage the landscape of the Yorkshire Dales?
6 (a) Describe the scene in Fig E. What has caused this damage?
   (b) What are the aims of the Three Peaks Project?

10 CASE STUDY FIVE: CENTER PARCS

Over 20 years ago, in Holland, I had a vision of how we could spend our leisure time.
A totally new concept. An experience the weather couldn't spoil. A holiday with every imaginable facility built in, combining the flavour of the country club, the health farm, the sports complex and the villa holiday.
This formula proved an enormous success on the Continent. Sherwood Forest, the first of the British Villages, has enjoyed equally spectacular success and has changed the face of holidays in Britain. Elveden Forest Holiday Village, the second Center Parcs village, was opened in August 1989 and is enjoying the same success as her sister village.

Piet Derksen
Chairman
Center Parcs International

Fig. A

Fig. B Center Parcs – holidays of the future?

Fig. C Inside the Swimming Paradise

Fig B shows part of Center Parc's Sherwood Forest Holiday Village in Nottinghamshire. The huge dome is the Subtropical Swimming Paradise where the temperature is a constant 84F and tropical vegetation thrives (Fig C). It is much more than a swimming pool, with wild water rapids, wave machine, waterslides, hot whirlpools and plenty of seats to sit and enjoy a drink or snack.

At the heart of the Center Parcs concept is the all-weather nature of the holiday:

Gone are the days of having to spend ages travelling hundreds, if not thousands, of miles to reach exotic holiday destinations where the temperatures are in the 80s Fahrenheit. At Center Parcs you can enjoy everything the tropics have to offer just a short distance away from your villa in all seasons.

Fig. D   From Center Parcs brochure

Apart from the dome there are many other sport and leisure facilities, restaurants and shops. 700 luxury villas provide the accommodation, dotted around the 440 acres of woodland and water (Fig D). The whole village cost £35m, which included the planting of over 300 000 new trees and shrubs. The village provides over 600 permanent jobs.

The Council for the Protection of Rural England has criticised Center Parcs. The Council's senior planner claims that Center Parcs denies open access to the forest and creates 'something wholly irrelevant to the experience of the countryside'.

Center Parcs obviously caters for a strong demand, however. Since the first Village was opened in 1967, 13 more have been built, seven in the Netherlands, two each in Britain and Belgium and one each in France and West Germany. Is the Center Parcs concept the shape of things to come in the British tourist industry?

QUESTIONS

1 (a) Describe what you can see in Fig B.
  (b) What are the tourist facilities at this site?
  (c) What type of tourist would be attracted to this site?
2 What are the advantages of a holiday at Sherwood Forest Holiday Village?
3 'At Center Parcs you can enjoy everything the tropics have to offer . . .'
  (a) Explain the basis for this claim.
  (b) Do you agree with the claim? If not, why not?
4 How has the Center Parcs Sherwood Forest Holiday Village been criticised?
5 The village provides 600 permanent jobs. Many other holiday centres provide only seasonal jobs. Why is Center Parcs different?
6 In groups of four, discuss the advantages and disadvantages of a Center Parcs holiday.

11 PLANNING A TOURIST COMPLEX

The island of Santa Maria is one of the few remaining Mediterranean islands to be little touched by tourism. However, this is about to change. The government has decided to build an airport and allow the development of tourist complexes on the island.

Your assignment

You work for New Horizon Travel Ltd. Your company is keen to be involved in Santa Maria's tourist development and has sent you to find out more about the island. Study the information. Then use it to:

1 Prepare a report for your company on the background to the development of tourism on Santa Maria. Consider the views of all interested parties, including local and national government, local people, businesses and environmental groups. Write your report in a series of numbered paragraphs. Each section must have a separate heading.

2 Prepare detailed plans for the development of the tourist complex at La Stancia. The plans must include the following:
- Map of the tourist complex including the hotel, apartment blocks, swimming pool, car park, access roads and marina.
- Details of each of the developments and of any anticipated engineering problems.
- A map of the island showing the infrastructural developments required eg improved road from the airport, increased water supply etc.
- Any environmental measures which you wish the company to consider adopting.

3 You should also include brief alternative strategies which you could use if the government decides not to approve the Los Trancos development. Where else could a complex be built? What would be the advantages and disadvantages of alternative sites?

A tourist complex featuring a hotel, associated apartment blocks, car park and swimming pool is to be built at La Stancia Bay on the island of Santa Maria. The four-star hotel will have 400 bedrooms and there will be accommodation for an extra 250 people in the apartment blocks. A small marina with 60 berths will be built on the western side of the bay.

Press release from New Horizon Travel

The plan to build a tourist complex at La Stancia Bay threatens one of the last remaining refuges of the loggerhead turtle. This remarkable reptile comes ashore only to lay her eggs. The female turtle climbs out of the water and makes her way up the sandy beach until she is above high water mark. Here she digs a hole and lays her eggs in it, carefully covering them with sand. They hatch out by the heat of the sun and the young turtles make straight for the sea. La Stancia Bay is a site of worldwide botanical importance.

Press release from the environmental group Greenpeace

An airport with a 2500 metre runway able to take all short- and medium-range jet airliners will be built at Los Trancos near Puerto Novo on the island of Santa Maria. The airport's terminal building will be able to handle one million passengers per year. A small cargo terminal will also be built for the island's agricultural produce, thus reducing dependence on shipping. The construction of the airport has been made possible by the plans of New Horizon Travel to build a tourist complex near La Stancia.

The government is of the opinion that tourism will provide much-needed employment and income for the island, allaying fears that the recent decline of the island's economy will worsen.

Government proposal to build an airport on Santa Maria

We must prepare ourselves to resist an invasion. An invasion of tourists will result if the airport plans are permitted to proceed. Noise, litter, congestion and crime accompany these unwelcome visitors. Do we really want Santa Maria to become like the Costa del Sol? A sea of concrete hotels and villas? Must our farming and fishing traditions be destroyed?

Extract from a letter to *El Mundo*, Santa Maria's local newspaper, by local resident Miguel Gonzalez

Gonzalez is wrong! Tourism must be our future. Our fishing fleet's catches have been falling in recent years. Several farmers have sold their land as large farms have increased in size. Where will the new jobs come from, if not from tourism? Tourism will bring money and new facilities to our island. The new airport should be built, and built quickly.

Extract from letter written in reply

We fully support the plans to build a hotel and tourist complex at La Stancia. We anticipate greatly increased trade as a result of the influx of tourists. We wish to co-operate in plans to develop a new shopping centre in Puerto Novo.

Statement from the Puerto Novo Shopowners' Association

The District authority supports the plan to build a new airport at Los Trancos. However, we are concerned at the runway alignment which will lead to aircraft taking off and landing over Puerto Novo with consequent noise problems and possible threats to public safety.

The authority is concerned at the siting of the proposed tourist complex at La Stancia Bay. We appreciate the environmental objections to this site and are of the opinion that Puerto Novo provides a more suitable site.

Statement from the Puerto Novo District local government authority

Headlines in the island's newspapers

27

SANTA MARIA

Area: 108 sq km

Population: 9000

Main settlements:
- Puerto Novo (4555 persons)
- La Stancia (2100 persons)

Main occupations: (1990 census figures)
- Fishing (340 employees)
- Fish processing (80 employees)
- Farming (440 employees)
- Shops (210 employees)
- Bars and cafes (88 employees)
- Garages (24 employees)

The passenger approaching the island of Santa Maria by boat from Menorca will be struck by the impressive limestone cliffs which rise sheer from the azure waters of the Mediterranean Sea. A wisp of cloud often shrouds the summit of Mount Centeneras.

After rounding Cabo Falcon, Santa Maria's softer side becomes apparent. Small fields and olive trees lie inland, behind broad, sandy beaches. The island's fertile plain has allowed a prosperous agriculture to develop. In recent years the traditional wheat and olives have been supplemented by oranges, melons, tomatoes and other salad crops, much of it in greenhouses. Competition with larger production areas on mainland Spain and in other parts of the European Community has recently hit the farmers' income and poses a threat to their future.

The boat docks at the small harbour of Puerto Novo. The stone harbour wall was built during the 19th century when the island's lime trade was at its height. The trade ended in the 1970s. Puerto Novo's harbour is now crowded with fishing boats and a variety of yachts. Tourism has touched Santa Maria surprisingly little. The lack of an airport means that package tours are kept at bay. There are no high-rise hotels or tourist complexes. Only those tourists able to travel by yacht arrive at the island. How long can Santa Maria's splendid isolation last?

Lesser known islands of the Mediterranean Hilary Clark (1989)

A peaceful island scene – but for how long?

28

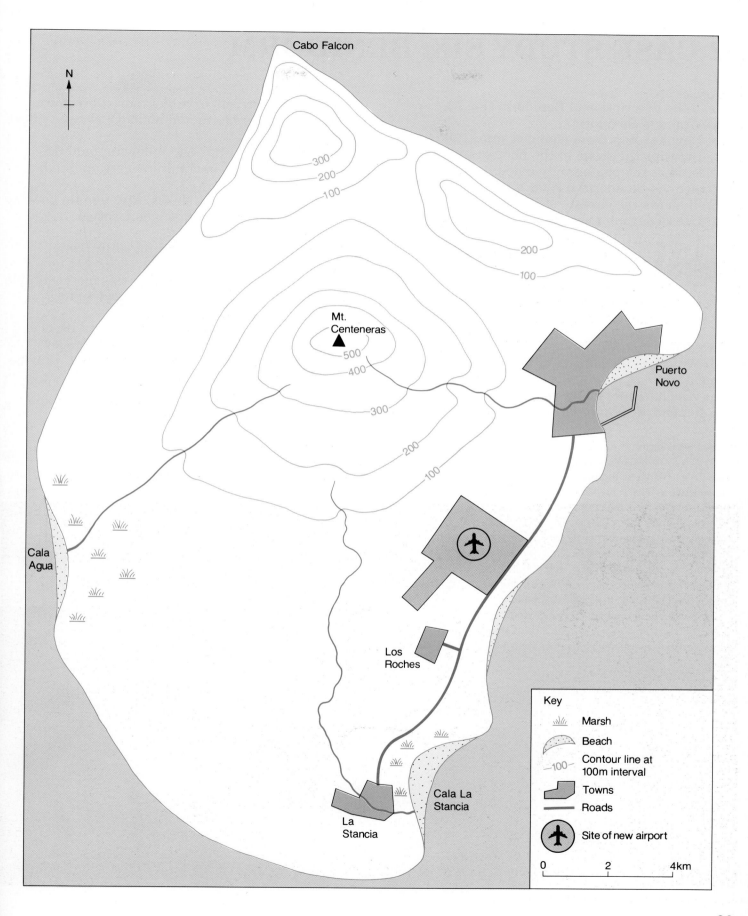

Cabo Falcon

N

300
200
100

200
100

Mt.
Centeneras

500
400
300
200
100

Puerto
Novo

Cala
Agua

Los
Roches

La
Stancia

Cala La
Stancia

Key

Marsh

Beach

—100— Contour line at
100m interval

Towns

Roads

Site of new airport

0   2   4km

12 CASE STUDY SIX: BENIDORM

1 Read the description of Benidorm (Fig A).
  (a) Where is Benidorm?
  (b) How has Benidorm changed since 1960?
  (c) Describe the scene in the photograph.
  (d) Look at the photograph and state what attractions Benidorm has for a tourist.
2 Fig B shows the climate of Benidorm.
  (a) Use the graph to complete the table below:

Month	J	F	M	A	M	J	J	A	S	O	N	D
Temperature °C	12	12	14							18	17	13
Rainfall mm		30	25	18						18	35	38

  (b) What is (i) the total rainfall (ii) the range of temperature?
  (c) Name (i) the two hottest months (ii) the two driest months.
  (d) Why does the climate of Benidorm attract tourists?
  (e) Which month would you choose for a holiday in Benidorm? Why?

Fig. A Benidorm

The Costa Blanca is the name given to 500 km of the Spanish coast between Denia and Almeria. Until the 1960s there was little tourist development here. Now it is Spain's leading holiday area. Nowhere shows the results of this boom more than Benidorm. Thirty years ago Benidorm was a small fishing village flanked by two crescent-shaped sandy beaches. Now it is the largest resort on the Costa Blanca with over 400 000 beds for tourists. There are hundreds of hotels, apartment blocks, shops, cafes, restaurants, discos and clubs. The towering skyline of Benidorm has earned it the nickname "Manhattan-on-the-Med". Rarely can a place have been so transformed in such a short time!

3 Study the extracts from the tourist brochure describing Benidorm and holidays at two typical hotels (Fig C).
  (a) Which hotel has the following facilities:
  (i) a pool table   (ii) children's cots and high chairs
  (iii) satellite TV film shows   (iv) ten-pin bowling
  (v) disco/bar   (vi) promenade location.
  (b) Which hotel is larger?
  (c) What is the Official Rating of the Hotel Selomar?
  (d) Which hotel would you say was more suitable for a family with two children aged 4 and 7 years? Why?
  (e) How long is the flight to the Costa Blanca from (i) Leeds (ii) Bristol (iii) Glasgow?
  (f) What further information does Fig C provide about the attractions of Benidorm?

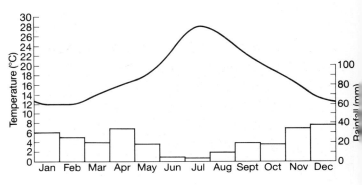

Fig. B   Climate of Benidorm

★ HOTEL PUEBLO ★

Most visitors aren't satisfied with just one visit to the Pueblo - they want to come back again and again. It's almost impossible to think of a facility that is missing in this friendly hotel. The whole family will feel more than welcome, whether it's the children playing crazy-golf, going on rides or enjoying their own playground, or the adults practising their ten-pin bowling or letting their hair down at Eva's bar. There's plenty of time for relaxation too - try the large sun terrace, or have a dip in one of the Pueblo's pools. The hotel's standards are kept high and its good reputation is well deserved.

* two swimming pools; attractive gardens and extensive sun terraces;
* full central heating ; bar service to pool
* comfortable bar/lounges
* Eva's disco/bar; daily Happy Hour
* all meals buffet-style; a la carte menu available; Christmas Day and New Year's Eve Gala meals included; snack bar
* tennis court (equipment for hire); table tennis
* TV lounge; games room; pool table; cards, chess
* shop
* children's section of swimming pool; playground; cots and highchairs available; Thomson Children's Rep and Big T Club

"Great value for a fun-packed holiday with an easy-going atmosphere."

Prices are based on full board in a room with two or three beds, with private bath, wc and balcony. Available at a reduction: 3rd adult only in room.
Official Rating: *
Hotel Bedrooms: 564
Lifts: 3
Hotel Tel No: 853154

★ !! NIGHTLIFE !! ★

In the early evening in Benidorm, bars are packed for the resort's universal Happy Hour. Later, it's on to one of the many discos until the early hours - Benidorm's nightlife is really in a league of its own. Of course one evening you should really go to town and spoil yourself - you can take one of our exciting evening excursions - try the Benidorm Palace with its glittering floorshow for instance or even chance your luck at the casino in Villajoyosa four miles west. Denia is quieter, of course, with a selection of bars and restaurants in the town itself.

★ !!THAT'S ENTERTAINMENT!! ★

At the Pueblo Benidorm enjoy:

★ Daytime activities programme including keepfit ★

★ darts ★ ten-pin bowling ★ crazy-golf ★ French bowls ★

★ Comprehensive evening entertainments programme ★

★ Video film show twice a week ★

FLIGHT DETAILS

You can fly to Costa Blanca from:

Gatwick	(2 hrs 15 mins)
Luton	(2 hrs 15 mins)
Stansted	(2 hrs 15 mins)
Bristol	(2 hrs 30 mins)
Cardiff	(2 hrs 30 mins)
B'ham	(2 hrs 30 mins)
E. Mids	(2 hrs 30 mins)
Manchester	(2 hrs 45 mins)
Leeds	(2 hrs 45 mins)
Newcastle	(3 hrs)
Glasgow	(3 hrs)

For full flight details see page 22 of the Price and Flight Guide

★ HOTEL SELOMAR ★

While the majority of Benidorm's hotels are set back from the beach, the recently refurbished Selomar is one of the few exceptions. It is almost literally 'on the beach', separated from the sand only by a pleasant promenade. It stands at the very edge of Benidorm's bustling Old Town. You can watch the passers-by from the hotel's pavement cafe, or join them in a stroll along the seafront. The hotel is extremely comfortable inside and, although some bedrooms have restricted views, there are excellent views of the sea from every public room, including the tastefully decorated ground-floor lounge. To one side is the bar, whose entertainments area really comes to life in the evening, while upstairs another cosy bar and lounge overlook the sea. For an even better view, take the lift to the seventh floor and climb a short flight of stairs to the roof - you'll find a little pool, wide sun terraces and absolutely glorious views.

★ small rooftop swimming pool with sun terrace and bar service
★ central heating throughout
★ two bar/lounges; coffee bar adjoining hotel
★ all meals buffet-style; Christmas Day and New Year's Eve Gala meals included
★ TV; cards
★ children's cots and highchairs available

Plus ★ *Plus* ★ *Plus* ★ *Plus*

★ Daily Happy Hour
★ regular big-screen satellite TV film shows
★ Entertainments most nights
★ One complimentary drink per person per holiday
★ Gala Dinner once a week with free glass of wine followed by entertainments
★ Young at Heart extras - see page 5

"A really first-class location for this lovely hotel."

Prices are based on half board in a room with two or three beds with private bath and wc. Available at a supplement: balcony with restricted view, balcony and sea view, single room with shower and wc.
Available at a reduction: 3rd adult only in room.
Official Rating: ★ ★ ★ ★
Hotel Bedrooms: 246
Lifts: 3

Hotel Tel. No: 855277

Fig. C   Extracts from Thompson Holiday Brochures

13 CASE STUDY SEVEN: ZERMATT

Fig. A Zermatt

In the last 15 to 20 years, the popularity of winter holidays has increased dramatically. This is a godsend for the travel industry: not only are more people travelling (or the same people travelling more often), but some of the expensive systems developed for summer holidays, such as airports and airliners, can now continue operating throughout the year. The first growth market in winter holidays, and still the most important, is skiing and winter sports.

High in the Swiss Alps the air is clear and cool. More importantly, for the Swiss tourist industry, there is plenty of firm, deep snow. Almost half the tourists who visit Switzerland each year go for winter holidays. The travel agents' shelves are packed with brochures offering winter sports at a wide range of resorts throughout the Alps. One of the most famous (and most expensive!) resorts is Zermatt (Fig A).

Zermatt was a small farming village before the growth of winter holidays changed its character forever during the 20th century. It was the spectacular setting of Zermatt which ensured its popularity, plus the range of skiing and other sports available there. The village is dominated by the majestic beauty of the Matterhorn, and surrounded by many other mountain peaks and glaciers. Zermatt became famous

as a winter playground for the rich during the 1920s. It has excellent ski-runs, including some very demanding slopes for expert skiers. Zermatt is a very high resort, so in years when there is a shortage of snow it is not as badly affected as some other Alpine resorts.

Zermatt has now been completely taken over by tourism (Fig B). There are countless hotels, chalets, restaurants, discos and bars. For the non-skier there is still plenty to see and do, including skating, curling, ice hockey, tobogganing, walking, swimming, sauna baths and shopping. Numerous cable cars carry people high up into the mountains; there is also a mountain railway. The busiest months are February and March, but Zermatt's magnificent scenery attracts tourists throughout the year.

For many of the smaller, less fashionable resorts, the winter season is a short one. They lack the facilities Zermatt offers; once the snow melts, there is nothing for tourists to do. In the Swiss Alps as a whole, hotel beds are occupied for an average of only 120 days a year. Chalets are rented or occupied for only a few winter months. The rest of the time they stand empty, but buildings and services have to be maintained and paid for. This under-use of facilities loses money. Jobs are also seasonal; many people who work in tourism are unemployed during the summer months.

The Alpine environment is fragile. The presence of millions of skiers is undoubtedly causing damage. Tourists are noisy, they leave litter and erode the mountain slopes. The ski lifts, ski tows and cable cars scar the mountain scenery. The most accessible ski-runs are crowded with people. Modern concrete buildings bring city lifestyles into this once remote and peaceful landscape.

QUESTIONS

1 Where is Zermatt?
2 How has the development of winter tourism affected Zermatt's character?
3 What factors make Zermatt a popular winter resort?
4 What does a winter holiday in Zermatt offer for a non-skiing tourist?
5 (a) What are the busiest months for tourism in Zermatt?
  (b) Why does Zermatt attract tourists throughout the year?
6 Study Fig C.
  (a) On an outline map of Europe, draw flow lines to show where the tourists visiting Zermatt come from.
  (b) Why do you think that few tourists come from Switzerland's neighbours, Austria and Italy?
7 (a) What is the average number of days that hotel beds are occupied across the Swiss Alps as a whole?
  (b) What effects does this under-use of facilities have?
8 How might the natural environment of the Alps be damaged by tourism?
9 Form a group to discuss the following:

Should the development of tourism in the Alps be controlled? If so, how could it be done and who should be responsible? Who would benefit? Who would suffer?

Country of origin	% of total foreign tourists
West Germany	42
USA	11
Netherlands	9
UK	9
France	8
Belgium	5
Sweden	4
Spain	2
Denmark	2
Others	8

Fig. C   Countries of origin of tourists visiting Zermatt

Fig. B   The ski slopes at Zermatt

14 CASE STUDY EIGHT: DISNEYWORLD

Almost everyone knows the name Walt Disney. You probably associate it with films, or with cartoon characters like Mickey Mouse or Donald Duck. In the early 1950s the giant Walt Disney Corporation decided to invest in a new area of entertainment: theme parks.

The first park, Disneyland, opened in California in 1955. Disneyland was so successful that the Corporation decided to open a second park, in Florida, called Disneyworld (Fig A).

Disneyworld covers 112 sq km of central Florida. It was built on land reclaimed from forest, lake and swamp. The project cost over $400 million to build. As its name suggests, Disney*world* is really a collection of parks on a variety of themes. It aims to provide something for everyone.

Today, Disneyworld is one of the world's most famous purpose-built tourist attractions. 15 million people visit Disneyworld each year. As well as the attractions on offer, other factors help ensure its success:

- *Location* Central Florida is a popular holiday destination for both Americans and foreign visitors. Many cheap package tours operate from Europe.

Fig. B   A rocket launch at Cape Canaveral

- *Climate* Florida's hot summers and warm winters attract visitors all year round. Europeans like the hot summers, Americans like the warm winters (especially if they come from the Northern USA, where winters can be severe).
- *Accessibility* Central Florida can be reached easily from other parts of the USA, and from Europe. There are many other attractions within easy reach of Disneyworld. These include the Kennedy Space Center at Cape Canaveral (Fig B), Sea World (the largest sea – quarium in the world) and the Wet' n Wild water sports park. A little further afield are the Everglades, the resorts of the Gulf Coast and Miami.

Fig C shows just some of the attractions of Disneyworld. Critics attack the resort as being purely escapist and artificial. They say that it paints too rosy a picture of the world and of technology. Others point to the large area of land covered by Disneyworld. This is destined to increase further as the resort grows. In 1989 New Pleasure Island, a night-time entertainment area, and the Disney-MGM Studios were opened. This strengthened Disneyworld's claim to be one of the world's top tourist attractions. The appeal of the Disney theme is such that in 1991 a new Disneyworld will open in France, near Paris. It will be the first Disney theme park outside the USA.

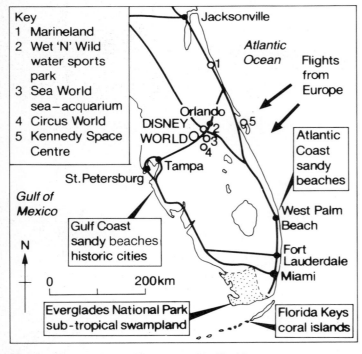

Key
1 Marineland
2 Wet 'N' Wild water sports park
3 Sea World sea – acquarium
4 Circus World
5 Kennedy Space Centre

Jacksonville
Atlantic Ocean
Flights from Europe
Orlando
DISNEY WORLD
Tampa
St.Petersburg
Gulf of Mexico
N
0   200km
Gulf Coast sandy beaches historic cities
Atlantic Coast sandy beaches
West Palm Beach
Fort Lauderdale
Miami
Everglades National Park sub-tropical swampland
Florida Keys coral islands

Fig. A   The location of Disneyworld in Florida

QUESTIONS

1 Where is Disneyworld?
2 Why is Disneyworld well located?
3 Use the photographs and text in Fig C to help you produce a brochure advertising the attractions of Disneyworld.
4 How has Disneyworld been criticised?
5 Disneyworld is one of the world's top tourist attractions. Do you think that its owners need to pay any attention to critics?

Fig. C   The attractions of Disneyworld

Magic Kingdom   A collection of fantasy theme parks ranging from *Adventureland's* Jungle Cruise to *Frontierland's* steamboat rides. Visitors can stroll along Main Street USA, a recreation of a turn-of-the-century town, and greet Mickey Mouse and Donald Duck in *Fantasyland*. The Skyway to Tomorrow train carries visitors to Space Mountain where they can take a trip to

(i) One of the Disneyworld paddlesteamers

Magic Castle

Epcot Center   This is an entertaining presentation of Earth's past, present and future brought to life in an amazing array of special effects. It includes *World Showcase* where visitors can experience the atmosphere of nine different countries.

Disney-MGM Studios   Opened in 1989, visitors can walk into the world of the movies for an inside view of behind-the-scenes action. They can watch movies being made, see the Disney cartoon animators at work, learn the secrets of special effects and even star in their own show at the Disney Television Centre.

(iii) Visitors can travel through the Epcot centre on a monorail

15 CASE STUDY NINE: EAST AFRICAN SAFARI

Fig. A

More tourists visit Kenya than any other country in tropical Africa. Although Kenya has attractive beaches and coastal resorts, it is the *safari* which attracts most tourists (Fig A). The Kenyan government has made tourist development a priority.

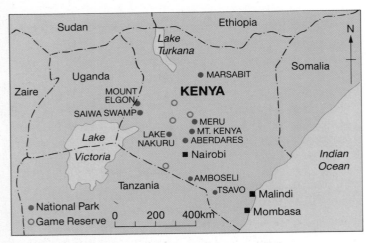

Fig. B Kenya's game reserves and national parks

It has spent money on building hotels, airports, safari lodges and all the other requirements for tourists from developed countries. The Boeings and Airbuses which land at Nairobi International Airport bring rich tourists from Europe, North America and Japan.

Kenya's splendid wildlife once attracted people whose idea of sport was to shoot animals. Fortunately today's shots are fired only by camera shutters! The government has banned game hunting since 1977, although illegal poaching continues. Fig B shows Kenya's reserves and national parks. Over 6% of Kenya's area is protected today.

Several hotels and lodges have been built in the protected areas. They have fully-furnished bedrooms, catering and bar facilities. Most have swimming pools. Some, like *Treetops* and *Mountain Lodge*, are built in the crowns of trees and on stilts. Elephant, buffalo, rhino and leopard come to drink at the waterholes beneath the tree lodges. Other tourists stay in tented camps. Land Rovers and minibuses drive the tourists in search of game to photograph. Some even travel in hot air balloons!

Tourism is an important source of income for Kenya. In 1987, for the first time, tourism took over from coffee as the country's number one foreign exchange earner. However, it is risky for a country to become over-dependent upon tourism. In 1982 there was an attempted military coup and in 1983 several armed attacks upon tourists. The bad publicity from these events seriously hit Kenya's tourist earnings. Since 1983 Kenya's tourist trade has resumed its spectacular growth. By 1988 the number of tourists had doubled from the 1983 figure (Fig C shows numbers of tourists visiting Kenya; Fig D shows where these tourists came from).

Year:	1981	1982	1983	1984	1985	1986	1987	1988
Tourists (thousands):	352	362	339	298	405	650	661	683

Fig. C   Number of tourists visiting Kenya 1981 – 1988

Unfortunately for Kenya, it is unlikely that the tourist industry can continue to grow at such a rapid pace. Kenya's game parks are already seriously overcrowded. Wildlife in the more popular, accessible parks such as Amboseli is harassed every day by mobs of safari tour mini-buses. The fragile vegetation is being seriously eroded. The animals are finding it difficult to pursue their natural lives.

Nationality	Percentage of total tourists
West German	19
British	12
US	10
Swiss	8
Scandinavian	8
Italian	6
Japanese	4
Canadian	2
Other	31

Fig. D   Nationality of tourists visiting Kenya

Tourism also clashes with the needs of Kenya's *human* population. Kenya has one of the fastest population growth rates in the world (Fig E). More mouths to feed means an increased demand for food crops – and farmland on which to grow them. This threatens the reserves and parks. Farmers searching for scarce arable land encroach on the parks. More land is ploughed up for crops each year. As a result, herds of cattle wander in search of new grazing land. They invade the parks and eat the grass and fodder that the wildlife depends on.

Poaching also threatens the wildlife in Kenya's parks. Organised poaching has seriously reduced the numbers of animals, particularly elephant and rhinoceros. Although poaching is strictly illegal, there is still a high demand for ivory and rhino horn.

Year:	1961	1966	1971	1976	1981	1986	1988
Population (millions):	7.3	9.6	11.9	13.8	17.4	21.1	22.9

Fig. E   The population of Kenya 1961-1988

There is clearly a limit to the number of tourists Kenya can accommodate for safari holidays. Already, many tourists are discouraged from going to Kenya because of stories of congestion and low numbers of wild animals. Tanzania, Kenya's neighbour, has more wildlife and is attracting increasing numbers of tourists. At present, it lacks the quality of accommodation and infrastructure that Kenya has, but Tanzania could well become a major competitor during the 1990s.

QUESTIONS

1 Why are tourists attracted to Kenya for a holiday?
2 Fig D shows the nationalities of tourists visiting Kenya.
   (a) Draw a divided bar or pie graph to illustrate these statistics.
   (b) Why do so many of the tourists visiting Kenya come from Europe, America and Japan?
3 Study Fig C.
   (a) Draw a line graph to illustrate these statistics.
   (b) Describe the changes in the number of tourists shown by the table.
   (c) What may explain these changes?
4 Why is it risky for a country to become over-dependent upon tourism?
5 Study Fig E.
   (a) Draw a bar graph to illustrate these statistics.
   (b) What effect might this rapid population growth have upon Kenya's tourist industry?
6 Form a group. You are a Kenyan family with several children, living beside the Tsavo National Park. You do not have enough land to support your growing family. You want to move on to land within the National Park to set up a farm. What will you say to the Kenyan National Parks Authority? What do you think they will reply?
7 (a) Why are some tourists now attracted to Tanzania rather than Kenya?
   (b) Discuss with your neighbour what the government of Tanzania will need to do if it is to develop its own tourist industry.

16 CASE STUDY TEN: THE METROCENTRE

A shopping centre may seem a strange subject to study in a book on travel and tourism. Yet, shopping is a major leisure activity. The potential of linking tourist facilities with shopping facilities has only recently been fully recognised.

The construction of out-of-town shopping centres has provided the spur for integrating shopping and leisure. Europe's largest such centre is at Gateshead. It is called the MetroCentre (Fig A). The MetroCentre first opened in 1986. There are over 350 shops here, including branches of most of Britain's largest retailers. The aim of the developers was to make a shopping visit to MetroCentre an enjoyable leisure activity and not a dreaded weekly chore. They planned that shoppers would spend considerably longer at the MetroCentre than at a normal shopping centre: it would be the site of day trips. In addition to shopping, visitors could eat a meal, watch a film, go ten-pin bowling and visit a theme park.

Fig. A   Inside the Metrocentre

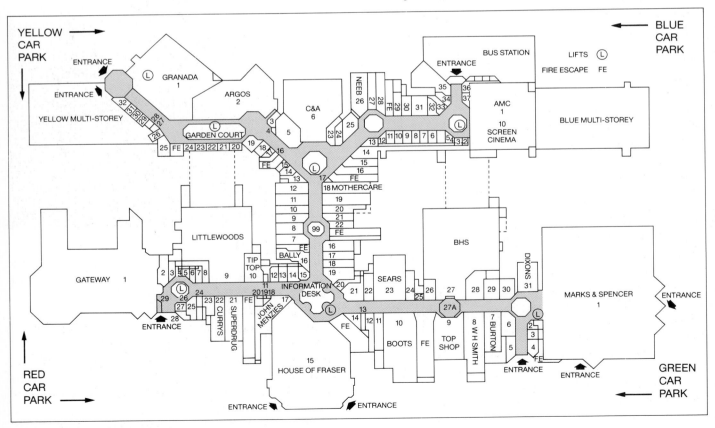

Fig. B   Plan of the Metrocentre

Fig. C *Metroland*

The MetroCentre has five long glass-roofed malls (Fig B). These connect the shops and enclose trees, tropical plants, waterfalls and fountains. In addition, there are specific leisure facilities:

- A ten-screen cinema complex
- A funfair/theme park called *Metroland, the Kingdom of King Wiz* (Fig C)
- A fitness centre
- A Medieval Village and Antique Village

The sheer size and space of the MetroCentre is what most impresses visitors. It covers 200 000 sq m. It was built on the site of an old coal ash tip. Its effects on the local economy and job market have been dramatic. 6000 new jobs have been created in one of the most depressed areas of Tyneside. An average of 300 000 people visit the MetroCentre each week. The attraction of the MetroCentre is so great that coaches visit it from as far away as Nottingham, Birmingham, Edinburgh and even Cheltenham!

The MetroCentre may be the prototype of shopping and leisure complexes in the future. However, none of the British centres is likely to match the West Edmonton Mall in Canada (Fig D). This is the world's largest shopping centre. Nearly 1000 shops are combined with a two-hectare water park featuring 22 waterslides and waves breaking on a palm-lined beach, an indoor amusement park with the world's longest roller coaster, four submarines and over 40 other rides, an ice rink and a zoo.

Fig. D   Edmonton Mall

QUESTIONS

1 (a) Where is the MetroCentre?
  (b) What is it?
  (c) Use the photographs to help you describe the appearance of the MetroCentre.
2 What was the aim of the developers of the MetroCentre?
3 Do you think the MetroCentre would be a good site for a day-trip? Why?
4 (a) Where is the world's largest shopping centre?
  (b) How does it compare with the MetroCentre?

17 A QUESTIONNAIRE SURVEY OF TRAVEL HABITS

Use the students at your school or college as a resource to study people's travel habits. Design a questionnaire to find out the information you need. Follow these steps:

1 The aims

First of all, decide what your survey is aiming to find out. It can be quite a simple aim, for example, to answer the question:

What are the most popular holiday destinations for students at .... School / College?

or a rather more complex aim, for example, to determine:

Is there any pattern to the types of holiday taken by people from different social classes?

2 What questions should you ask?

Two important things to remember:
- Make sure that the questions you ask are easily understood and will obtain the information which you seek.
- Do not ask too many questions – no more than seven.

3 Drawing up your questionnaire

Work in groups of three or four. Decide on six or seven questions designed to help you answer the question:

Is there any pattern to the types of holiday taken by people from different social classes?

First, you need to agree on what you *mean* by social class, and how you can define what social class a person belongs to. Some things that can give a good indication are:
- the type of job a person does
- the area in which they live (Think about where you live. In which areas are the larger, detached houses? They will belong to fairly wealthy people. Less well-off people will probably live in the council house areas, or areas of older terraced housing near the town centre.)
- the newspapers people read (Wealthier, middle-class people usually read 'quality' newspapers such as *The Times*, the *Guardian* or the *Independent*. Less wealthy, working-class people often read tabloid newspapers such as the *Sun*, *Daily Mirror* or the *Star*.)

You could combine these questions with questions about people's travel habits (see Fig A).

A QUESTIONNAIRE OF TRAVEL HABITS

1 Where did you go for your most recent holiday?

    Location (town, city): ....

    County/region: ....

    Country: ....

2 How long did you stay?

    LESS THAN A WEEK / ONE WEEK /

    TWO WEEKS / OVER TWO WEEKS

3 Who organised your holiday?

    YOUR FAMILY / TRAVEL AGENT /

    TRAVEL COMPANY /

    OTHER (please specify) ....

4 What type of holiday was it?

    VISITING FRIENDS OR RELATIVES /

    BEACH / ACTIVITY / TOURING/

    OTHER (please specify) ....

5 Where do you live? (Street name needed) ....

    ....

6 What are your parents' (guardians') jobs? ....

    ....

7 What newspapers are read at your home? ....

    ....

Fig. A

4 Conducting the survey

There are a lot of students in your school or college. You do not have time to question them all. You need to question a *sample* number of students. The larger the sample of students you can question, the more detailed your information will be. A minimum of 30 students should be questioned – preferably 50 or even 100. If you work in groups, you can complete this task more quickly.

Work in pairs to carry out the survey. Ask people politely if they would mind answering your questions, and remember to thank them afterwards. Do not get upset if they refuse – that is their right. Simply thank them and find someone else.

5 Presenting the data

You now have 30 (or 50 or 100) completed questionnaires. What are you going to do with the answers you have obtained? The first thing is to record the answers to each of the questions, for example:

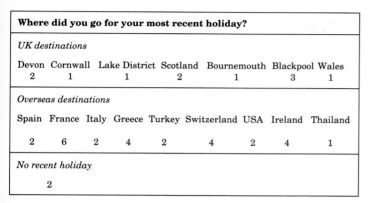

Where did you go for your most recent holiday?						
UK destinations						
Devon	Cornwall	Lake District	Scotland	Bournemouth	Blackpool	Wales
2	1	1	2	1	3	1
Overseas destinations						
Spain	France	Italy	Greece	Turkey	Switzerland	USA	Ireland	Thailand
2	6	2	4	2	4	2	4	1
No recent holiday						
2						

You can present your results in a variety of ways, such as bar graphs (Fig B), pie graphs (Fig C), divided bars or a flow-line map (Fig D). Choose the way you think looks best and communicates the information most effectively.

6 Analysing the data

Study your results carefully. Use the questions as the basis for your analysis. What do the answers tell you?
- Which were the most popular destinations?
- What proportion of holidays were taken overseas?
- What was the average length of time spent on a holiday?
- Is there any pattern to the holiday destinations and the area in which the people live, or the jobs which they do?
- Are the results what you expected? If not, why not?

7 Conclusions

Write a summary of your survey. Explain what you were investigating and how you went about it. What results did you obtain?

Have you answered the question you posed at the start:

Is there any pattern to the types of holiday taken by people from different social classes?

How could you improve your study? What would you do differently if you repeated the survey?

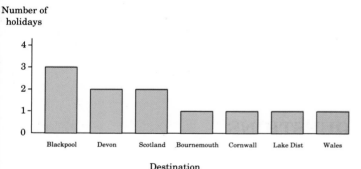

Fig. B   Bar graph showing UK destinations of holidaymakers in the sample survey

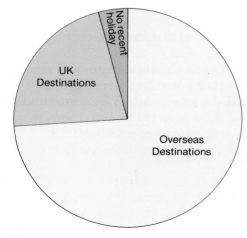

Fig. C   Where did you go for your most recent holiday?

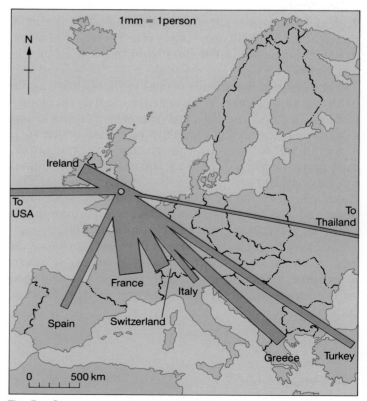

Fig. D   Overseas destinations of holidaymakers in the sample survey

41

18 WHAT IS CULTURE?

CULTURE *noun*
1. The total of the inherited ideas, beliefs, values and knowledge, which constitute the shared bases of social action.
2. The artistic and social pursuits, expression, and tastes valued by a society.

Fig. A   (From *The New Collins Concise Dictionary*)

The dictionary definition of culture may be a little difficult to understand, but this is because culture is not an easy term to define. Yet 'culture' is an important tourist attraction. For example, many foreign tourists are attracted by what they think of as British 'culture'. This may mean many things (Fig B).

Most of the attraction of British culture to foreign tourists is historical, but there is much about modern Britain which also attracts visitors. It is important to identify what is culturally important in order to promote it and make it available to tourists – and also to protect it, as in the case of Stonehenge (see Unit 8).

It is difficult to judge how much a building will appeal to tourists simply by looking at it (or at a picture like Fig F). Tourists are often more interested in what happened in the past than in what a place is like today.

For example, thousands of people visit Corfe Castle, in Dorset, every year. They are attracted by its bloody history. In 978 King Edward (the Martyr) was killed at Corfe, on the orders of his mother. Visitors can see a memorial to him in the village square. Later, during the English Civil War, the castle was besieged by Parliamentary troops for many weeks. The Royalists were led by a woman, Lady Bankes. They defended the castle strongly, but eventually it fell and was blown up by the Parliamentarians.

The fact that Corfe Castle is in ruins increases its appeal to tourists. The ruins provide a more atmospheric setting and a reminder of the violence which once shattered the peace of the Dorset countryside.

- a visit to a theatre to see a play by Shakespeare
- a pub
- a cricket test match
- an historic site such as the Tower of London or Stonehenge
- a street market
- an attractive town or city such as Chester, Winchester, Norwich or Durham
- the Edinburgh Festival

Fig. B

QUESTIONS

1 Study the four photographs (Figs C to F). List the features in each which are culturally important.
2 Which of the two castles shown in Figs E and F do you think would appeal most to tourists? Give your reasons.
3 Give your own definition of:
   (a) British culture (b) American culture (c) French culture.
4 (a) How do Corfe Castle's historical connections increase its appeal to tourists?
   (b) How could Corfe's history be communicated to visitors? List your ideas, and say which you think would be the most effective?

Fig. C   Scene from *Torchlight and Laser Beams*, a play produced at the Edinburgh Festival

Fig. D   Morris dancers in a Yorkshire village

Fig. E   Harlech Castle

Fig. F   Corfe Castle and village

43

19 HOW TOURISM HAS IMPINGED UPON LIFE IN YORK

This magnificent, medieval walled city must surely rank second only to London, our capital, in historical importance ... but in aesthetic terms some people place it first in its own right. Many cities have major attractions, but York is the total experience ... it is thought by many to be the ultimate in terms of amount, importance and variety of history and attractions.

Fig. A *The Discovery Guide to the Historic City of York*, M. Parker and P. Grant, 1989

York is one of Britain's most important tourist centres (Fig A). The city is just two hours from London by High Speed Train, and it has good road and rail links with other parts of Britain.

Every year about 2.5 million people visit York. They are attracted by the city's famous buildings (Fig B) and its history. Parts of York seem to have changed very little since medieval times, like The Shambles (Fig C). The inner city is surrounded by 5km of the best-preserved medieval walls in Britain. York Minster is one of the country's most famous cathedrals (Fig D).

Fig. C The Shambles

Fig. B Mansion House, York

Tourism provides thousands of jobs in York. Many people work in facilities provided for tourists: museums such as York Castle Museum, the Yorkshire Museum, the National Railway Museum, the Jorvik Viking Centre, the York Story and the Yorkshire Museum of Farming; the York City Art Gallery; historic buildings open to the public; shops, pubs and restaurants. It is easy to gain an impression of York as a kind of living museum, a city preserved only for the tourists. Yet York has a population of 100 000 people. It is a modern industrial centre, famous for its sweet factories (Rowntrees and Terry's), railway workshops, and university.

Tourism places constraints on development in York. In 1989 plans to build the national headquarters of the National Curriculum Council were delayed by the discovery of an important Roman building on the site. The developers threatened to abandon the project and build in another town, thus depriving York of valuable jobs and income. In the end, an alternative site was made available.

There has been conflict between tourism and the residents of York. York Minster's record for visitors is 18 000 in a single day! Tourists crowd the city's narrow streets, fill its car parks and shops, create

Fig. D York Minster

noise and litter. During the summer, residents of the old city cannot park their cars outside their own houses. The large number of tourists sometimes threatens to destroy the atmosphere of York – the atmosphere the tourists have come to seek.

QUESTIONS

1 Use an atlas to help you describe the location of York and its position in relation to other cities. How accessible is York?

2 Using the photographs to help you, describe the attractions of York for tourists.

3 'It is easy to gain an impression of York as a kind of living museum, a city preserved only for the tourists.' What evidence is there that this impression is false?

4 (a) What percentage of the visits to York are day-trips? (Fig E)

(b) Why are day-trips so predominant?

5 Study Fig F. What does this suggest about York's tourist appeal?

6 How does tourism affect the life of those who live in the city?

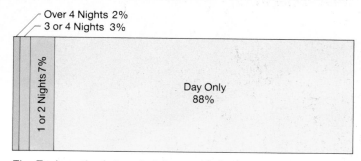

Fig. E Length of stay of visitors to York

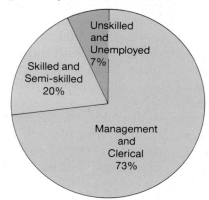

Fig. F Occupation of the head of household of York's tourists

45

20 THE CULTURAL HERITAGE OF SPAIN

Fig. A

If you asked a group of British tourists to describe Spanish 'culture', they might mention high-rise hotel blocks, cheap alcohol, donkey rides, oily food... It is possible for British people who visit Spanish resorts like Benidorm or Palma Nova to remain insulated within their own culture: pubs, discos, fish and chips, British videos.

The photographs in Fig A show different aspects of Spanish culture. Tourists who explore no further than the beach resorts of the Costas, such as Torremolinos and Benidorm, see little of the *real* Spain. Yet most tour companies offer holidaymakers the chance to travel inland, even if they stay at the coast. An increasing number of tourists take holidays away from the Costas, exploring Spain's rich cultural heritage.

The Spanish Tourist Authority has launched a campaign to promote holidays in the interior of the country (Fig B) and in cities like Barcelona (Fig C). It aims to appeal to a more 'discerning' type of tourist. Such tourists tend to spend more money than package tour visitors. The Spanish Tourist Authority hopes to spread the benefits of tourism more equally, and boost the economy of the poorer rural areas. Tourist income will also provide for the maintenance and conservation of historic sites.

Spain has a long and glorious history. Throughout Southern Spain the influence of the Moors is apparent. These Arab people ruled Spain for seven hundred years from the 8th century until they were finally defeated in 1492. Several notable buildings survive from the Moorish period, including the Alhambra at Granada and the Great Mosque at Cordoba. Great castles are found throughout Spain, bearing witness to centuries of warfare. Some of the castles have even become hotels.

There is far more to Spanish culture than its history. Spain offers rich and varied eating and drinking. Paella is a well-known dish. It consists mainly of rice coloured yellow with locally-grown saffron. Paella valenciano has fried pork, chicken and vegetables. Paella alicantina adds prawns, crab, octopus and lemon. The name 'paella' comes from the large iron pan in which the rice is cooked.

Another element of Spanish culture is its handicrafts: leather goods, rugs, basket-work, lace and pottery. In the coastal resorts prices are high and the goods may be of poor quality. The best bargains can be found inland, away from the Costas.

Bullfights remain an important part of Spanish culture. So does folk dancing. Most people know the dramatic flamenco, performed to the crashing rhythm of castanets, guitars and heels, but there are many other traditional dances. Many fiestas and festivals take place throughout Spain, both religious and traditional. Spain also possesses a rich contemporary culture, perhaps best seen in the streets of Barcelona.

Fig. B

QUESTIONS

1 Study the photographs in Fig A and describe what each shows.
2 (a) Why are increasing numbers of tourists being attracted to the interior of Spain, away from the main coastal resorts?
 (b) What are the benefits of this trend for Spain?
3 Read the *Independent* article (Fig C).
 (a) List the cultural attractions of Barcelona.
 (b) What sort of tourist would be attracted to Barcelona?
 (c) What benefits will tourists bring to Barcelona?
4 You are a travel company representative in Torremolinos. You have been told to arrange excursions to give your clients a taste of Spanish culture. Design the itinerary for three such excursions and justify your choice of activities. Bear in mind that excursions are increasingly activity-based. You will need to study a map of Spain, and to do some research into the cultural heritage of Andalucia, especially the Moorish influence in the region.

EUROPE'S MOST EXCITING CITY

Barcelona – the most stimulating city in Europe today and one of the easiest and cheapest to get to and stay in. The crowds who by-pass Barcelona on the way to the over-run Costas are missing the biggest holiday treat they could have had. This is Spain, but not only Spain. It is also Catalonia, a proud ancient kingdom that still puts its culture and language first on all the official signs.

Barcelona is Europe's pre-eminent fashion city – after Paris. Although this has little relevance to those who don't dress in £1,000 suits, the effect permeates down, giving popular shops a style and flair. Several large indoor arcades full of elegant boutiques have been built recently.

Shops, restaurants and hotels line the roads that run either side of the central promenade with its dozens of newspaper kiosks, flower and bird stalls, shoeshine stands, fortune-tellers, palmists, fire-swallowers, artists and, at the far end, a market for arts and crafts.

Barcelona is one of the few cities where crowds make pilgrimages just to look at the work of architects, especially those of the turn-of-the-century art nouveau movement. Their Modernist buildings give Barcelona a flair and excitement unmatched by any other major European city. Picasso grew up in Barcelona and two museums, the Picasso and the Museum of Modern Art, feature his work and that of his contemporaries.

adapted from a series of articles by Elkan Allen in
the *Independent*
12/13/14/15 April 1988

Fig. C   Barcelona, centre of Spanish culture

21 THE IMPACT OF TOURISM ON FLORENCE

Fig. A   Location of Florence

Read the travel guide description of Florence (Fig B). Use it and the photographs in Fig C to help you answer the following questions:

You must take Florence for what it is: one of history's phenomena. Few nations, let alone cities, can boast such an overpowering array of talent – literary, artistic, political – concentrated over so short a period of time. The names of some of Florence's greatest sons – Leonardo da Vinci, Michelangelo, Dante – are well known the world over.

Florence is much more than a museum of stone, marble and bronze. Its historic palaces, its great churches, its innumerable works of art are not dry as-dust relics. They're very much lived-in, worked-in, prayed-in and prized by today's Florentines.

Walking through this amazing city is likely to give you a pain in the neck, literally. There's so much to look at, simultaneously and at every level. You won't feel that time has stood still here. The centre's bustle, its noisy, smelly traffic, are very much part of the late 20th century. Yet most of the city's main streets are as narrow and their paving as uneven as they've ever been...

Fig. B   Extract from the *Berlitz Travel Guide to Florence*.

Fig. C   Some of Florence's major tourist attractions

QUESTIONS

1 Where is Florence?

2 Name the river flowing through Florence.

3 List the attractions of Florence for the tourist.

4 What problem does the Berlitz Guide (Fig B) hint at in present-day Florence?

5 Read the *Guardian* article (Fig D).
   (a) When was this article written?
   (b) Describe the problems facing Florence under the following headings:
      (i) Too many tourists   (ii) Too much traffic
      (iii) Changing the character of the city.

6 Read the *Observer* article (Fig E).
   (a) When was this article written?
   (b) What important change has occurred since the *Guardian* article was written?
   (c) What differences does William Scobie observe?
   (d) Which group of people in Florence do not approve of the change?
   (e) What problem does Scobie say has not been reduced?

7 Figs D and E give the same figure for the population of Florence, but they differ widely over the number of tourists.
   (a) What is the population of Florence?
   (b) What are the numbers given for tourists in (i) Fig D and (ii) Fig E?
   (c) Can you explain the difference between the two sources?
   (d) How would you try to check the figures? Where could you go to find an accurate figure?

8 (a) Do you think that the traffic control measures in Florence are justified?
   (b) Should any efforts be made to limit the number of tourists visiting Florence? How could this be done? What problems would it create?

What can be done to save the centre of Florence? The city groans under the weight of another summer's tourist invasion. Foot passage across the Ponte Vecchio is almost at a standstill. Along the cobbled embankment by the Arno traffic snarls and sprints as soon as the lights change and the narrow pavement, scarcely wide enough for two, is given over to a perpetual game of chicken as pedestrians try to force people coming the other way to step into the racetrack of a road.

With a population of half a million, Florence receives four times that number of people every year, each person staying on average three nights. Despairing Florentines say the overcrowding is making the city almost unliveable. An extension of the tourist industry will push out the last artisans and craftsmen and their families and end a tradition which goes back to the Renaissance and beyond.

'What tourists come to see is what our ancestors made for themselves. It was not made for tourists. The danger is that tourism may turn Florence into a high-class Disneyland,' says a member of the city council.

Florence belongs to the world. The world should worry about what is happening here.

Fig. D Extract from the *Guardian* newspaper 2/8/86

FLORENCE BRAKES THE CAR HABIT

I had no pass. So Florence, as long as I sat behind the steering wheel, was not for me. I got out and walked.

For the past month Florence has been a closed city for cars. Only the few remaining residents of the 'historic centre' – virtually the whole city – can drive in, along with taxis, buses, scooters and bicycles.

The difference is wondrous. For the first time in a difficult, 30-year love affair with Florence, last week I actually saw the calm, deliciously erratic piazza that lies before Santa Maria Novella's green and white marble facade. It was a revelation. I was there alone, as it were, with pigeons, pensioners, children, grass, tourists – or, as the poor lost things had become, coach-less, following the flag on foot, pilgrims.

Gone were the 600-odd triple-parked cars, the roaring rancorous flow that for decades has made hideous and dangerous the true heart of Italy. Banished are the giant, honking, belching killer coaches that usually park in solid ranks along the Arno's banks. More than a thousand of these Viking-packed monsters converge each day on Florence in the season.

Poor, besmirched Florence has been falling apart for decades. It is the worst city in Italy for acid rain – that wrecker of marble – caused by car exhausts.

This revolution has not been achieved entirely without violence. The merchants of Florence complain bitterly that business is being ruined. They threaten strikes, closures and blackouts. But recent polls show that nine out of ten Florentines, the young especially, welcome this war on the car.

The pedestrianisation of Florence will not lessen the tourist hordes, the sweating queues for the Uffizi Gallery, the mob scenes in Santa Croce. This summer, pouring over the Alps in the path of Goth, Vandal and Hun, nearly seven million trippers will invade a town of 500 000 – 14 tourists for every resident.

Fig. E Extracted from the article 'Florence brakes the car habit' by William Scobie in *The Observer* 1988

22 TOURISM, RELIGION AND CULTURE – ISLAM

Religion is an important aspect of culture. The buildings and art of Christianity are major tourist attractions today. In York, for example, the Minster is a major attraction (see Unit 19); in Florence the vast Duomo cathedral (which can hold over 20 000 people) is a must for any visitor. In Florence too you can gaze on some of the finest works of Christian painting by Fra Angelico, Botticelli, Giotto and Leonardo da Vinci in the Uffizi gallery.

Religious shrines and sites such as Lourdes in France and Knock in the Irish Republic, provide sites for pilgrimages by Roman Catholics. These religious visitors support many jobs in the local economy. Lourdes is one of the most visited single sites in France.

The Islamic world provides a different kind of religious experience. Istanbul in Turkey provides Europe's best example of an Islamic culture. Istanbul's fashionable shopping streets and restaurants seem familiar to Western eyes, but only a few streets away it is possible to glimpse a different culture. Istanbul's skyline is dominated by the sleek minarets and domes of a hundred mosques. From the minarets the priests call the Islamic faithful to prayer. St Sophia (Fig A) was a Christian church for over 900 years.

Fig. A   St Sophia. Once a church – now a mosque

Fig. B(i)   The magnificent interior of the Blue Mosque

Fig. B(ii)   The Blue Mosque

Fig. C   Moslem women in traditional dress

When the Turks conquered the city in 1453 they converted the church into a mosque. Minarets were added, rising above the enormous dome. Arabic writing, highlighted in gold, was placed around the apex of the dome. The writing consists of quotations from the holy book of Islam, the Koran. Further panels inscribed in Arabic with Islamic holy names are placed throughout the building. In 1935 St Sophia became a museum and now it is possible to see Christian frescoes and mosaics alongside Islamic decorations.

Two of the most famous mosques in Istanbul are the Blue Mosque (Fig B) and the Mosque of Suleiman the Magnificent. These bear little resemblance to a Christian church. Inside the Blue Mosque are over 20 000 blue ceramic tiles carrying floral decoration and Arabic writing. A white marble niche shows the direction of Mecca. The forecourt has a large fountain in its centre, where worshippers wash, and is surrounded by colonnades roofed with a series of small domes.

Turkey was Westernised during the 1920s. Among other things this meant that the Islamic religion was no longer allowed to intervene in government. Women no longer had to wear traditional dress with a veil. In many other Islamic countries Islamic law remains an integral part of the government. This is the case in Morocco. One result is that all religious buildings in the country are closed to non-Moslems, thus making Morocco less interesting for the tourist than it might otherwise be. However, there is the advantage of seeing people in traditional Islamic dress (Fig C). Visitors to Moslem countries are expected to respect the rules of the religion (Fig D).

JORDAN: A country rich in the relics of Greek, Roman and Islamic civilisations and as yet does not suffer from people pollution. Being a Moslem country you should observe local customs with regard to dress both off and on the beach. As a tourist you are not subject to regulations which affect the consumption of alcohol.

UNITED ARAB EMIRATES AND OMAN: Tourism is relatively new in this part of the world particularly in Oman. It is therefore extremely important that respect be shown to Moslem customs, especially when it comes to dress. Dress is informal, but ladies please nothing less than both halves of the bikini at the pool or on the beach. In town, skirts or slacks with tops well covered.

Fig. D   Quotations from the Kuoni *Worldwide* brochure

QUESTIONS

1 In what ways does religion provide attractions for tourism in Britain?

2 Find out about Lourdes in France. Carry out research in your school or college library. Large encyclopaedias will be a good starting point.
Why do Roman Catholics visit the site? What sort of tourist industry has developed at Lourdes?

3 Using the photographs and the text to help you, discuss the role of religion in the cultural differences you see between Britain and Turkey.

4 Read the descriptions from a holiday brochure given in Fig D. In what ways do you think that the Islamic culture of these countries affects European tourists?

23 TOURISM REACHES THAILAND

Welcome to the Kingdom of Siam (now known as Thailand), to the beautiful 'Land of Smiles', where a magical combination of fairytale palaces, awe-inspiring temples, spectacular beaches and stunning scenery combine with the natural friendliness of the Thai people to create a holiday destination that is hard to beat. Everyone will want to visit the incredible capital, Bangkok, with its famous palaces and temples, the majestic Chao Phya River, the shopping and the nightlife.

Fig. A   From Kuoni *Worldwide* brochure

What could be better than a holiday in Thailand (Fig A)? It is one of the long-haul (far off) destinations which have become increasingly popular with British holidaymakers who seek something more exotic than the Mediterranean can offer (Fig B). The tropical forests, spectacular beaches and unique culture are an attractive mixture.

70% of Thai people are rice farmers. The Thai government is keen to develop tourism to earn foreign exchange and provide wider job opportunities. Three million tourists visit Thailand each year, and over 1.5 million Thais have jobs in the tourist industry. Tourism has become Thailand's major foreign exchange earner.

Most tourists visit Thailand as part of a package tour, offered by one of the major travel companies. Such tours, with names like 'An Oriental Experience' or 'An Asian Affair', are multi-centre holidays. Typical itineraries (routes) are:
- Bangkok 3 nights, South Thailand and Malaysia 7 nights, Singapore 3 nights
- Kuala Lumpar 3 nights, Singapore 3 nights, Penang 4 nights, Bangkok 4 nights
- Singapore 3 nights, Bali 4 nights, Hong Kong 3 nights, Bangkok 4 nights, Pattaya 7 nights

Outside Bangkok, the main tourist centres in Thailand are the beach resorts of Pattaya, Hua Hin and Phuket and the northern resort of Chiang Mai, the ancient capital of Siam (Fig C). Chiang Mai was developed during the 1980s to relieve the increasing pressure of tourists on Bangkok. An international airport has been opened and many hotels have recently been built. Chiang Mai's attractions include ancient temples and a great bazaar where village craftsmen sell intricate teak carvings, silver and silk goods.

Fig. B   Thailand appeals to tourists seeking a more exotic holiday

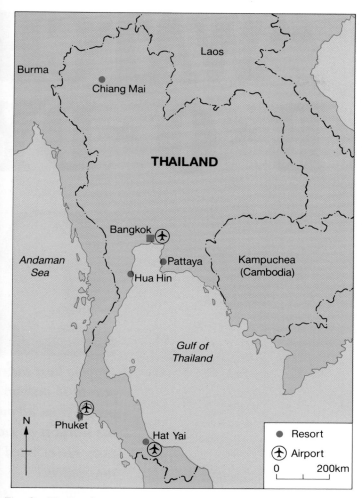

Fig. C   Thailand

And if the soul of this land
is behind the tourist poster
beckoning to sun, sea and sand,
it is equally there in the gutter...

Cheap pineapple and tropical
splendour you now enjoy, dear
traveller, is paid with impossible
lives lived out in unspeakable squalor.

C. Rajendra

Fig. D   A poet's view of the conflict between culture and tourism in Thailand

These countries are the tour operator's ideal. We really do not know of many hitches. Apart from traffic-jams in Bangkok, the odd pickpocket and the booming red light district in Bangkok and Pattaya that some people may find offensive... everything is as close to perfect as possible.

Fig. E   From Kuoni *Worldwide* brochure

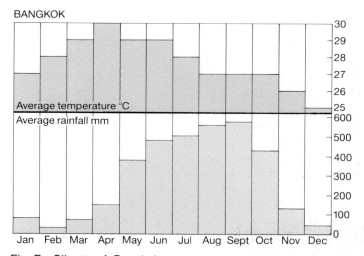

Fig. F   Climate of Bangkok

The impact of Western tourism on Thailand has not been totally beneficial. The tourist brochures extol the virtues of Thailand's tourist attractions. There is scarcely a mention of the vast sex industry which has developed in association with tourism. Bangkok and Pattaya have two of the world's most notorious red-light areas (ie districts where prostitutes and sex shows operate). Male tourists outnumber female tourists by two to one. Many of them are drawn to Thailand by the sex industry. In Bangkok alone there are an estimated 200 000 female prostitutes. They work in massage parlours, bars, escort agencies and shops. Many of the girls are migrants from the poverty-stricken farming areas of the north. A prostitute can earn at least ten times the wages of a waitress. The sex industry earns a high proportion of Thailand's tourist income. Without it, tourism would decline. Is this why the Thai government does little to control the sex industry? In Fig D a Thai poet writes about what he sees as the true cost of tourism.

You have to look very carefully to find a mention of Thailand's sex industry in travel brochures (Fig E).

QUESTIONS

1 Where is Thailand?
2 Use the photographs to help you describe the tourist attractions of Thailand.
3 Why has the Thai government been keen to develop the tourist industry?
4 (a) Name the main tourist resorts in Thailand. Give the main attraction of each one.
  (b) Study Fig F. Which would be the best months to visit Bangkok?
5 The sex industry can be viewed by some as 'local colour'. The Thai government has taken few measures to control it. Do you think that it should.?
6 Read the poem (Fig D).
  (a) What message does the poem have for Western tourists visiting Thailand?
  (b) Does the poet think that Thailand would be better off without tourism? Do you agree?

24 BODY LANGUAGE

Different cultures have different codes of communication. This is one of the things that makes foreign travel interesting – but it can also be hazardous!

One of the places where people from many different cultures meet and interact is an airport. BAA, operator of Heathrow airport, ran an advertising campaign focusing on body language – it illustrates just some of the possibilities for confusion.

QUESTIONS
1 Read the advertisement carefully. List how the following nationalities interpret the 'ring' gesture, made with thumb and forefinger.
(a) American (b) Japanese (c) French (d) Tunisian (e) Colombian
2 Form a group of four. Discuss how we all use and intepret body language in our everyday lives.
(a) Split into pairs. Each pair should devise a series of simple gestures with meanings known only to themselves.
(b) The two pairs in each group rejoin. Each pair then acts out a simple role-play, using their agreed gestures.
(c) The two pairs should then attempt to communicate with each other using their own gestures and no speech.
(d) How successful were your efforts to communicate by gesture alone?
3 Design some signs and symbols for an international airport which will be understood by all passengers.

"WATCH
B*O*DY

Playing host each year to 36 million people from all over the world is no easy task. Here, noted manwatcher Desmond Morris treats us to a light hearted look at some of the deadly, but unintentional, gaffes that can so easily occur when cultures collide at Heathrow the world's premier international airport. To find out more about the eye pull, the ear-tug, and the celebrated Greek 'moutza', now read on....

YOUR LANGUAGE?"

I'm never bored at airports. Quite the reverse. I visit them like other people go to the ballet. To a Manwatcher, there's nothing more fascinating than observing citizens of different countries mingling and exchanging body signals.

And nowhere is the performance so enjoyable as at Heathrow, the world's top international airport.

Day and night they pour in, a cast of 36 million a year from every corner of the globe.

Where else but Heathrow could you hope to see Brazilians rubbing shoulders with Brahmins, Poles with Polynesians, Madagascans with Minnesotans and Neapolitans with Nepalese?

**Intelligence or stupidity?
It depends whether you're Dutch.**

Each nationality has its own language of posture and gesture. But since these body-lingos are often mutually incomprehensible, an innocent gesture made in an airport lounge may well be an unwitting insult.

Something in your eye? Think before you touch the lower lid. If a Saudi sees you, he'll think you're calling him stupid, but a South American senorita will think you're making a pass at her.

There is no greater insult you can offer a Greek than to thrust your palms towards his face. This gesture,

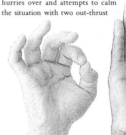

called the 'moutza,' is descended from the old Byzantine custom of smearing filth from the gutter in the faces of criminals as they were led in chains through the city.

So vile is this insult that in Greece even the Churchillian Victory-V is taboo, as it looks like a half-'moutza.'

Thus the Cretan or Athenian traveller, ordering two teas in a Heathrow restaurant, will carefully reverse his palm and give the waiter two fingers in the best

...means five ...ent ...s (four ...m ...ing) ...e ...ent ...ries.

Harvey Smith manner. With 22,600 orders for cups of tea open to misinterpretation every day, the wonder is the place functions at all.

It's so easy to give offence. Suppose a passenger asks at the Information Desk where he should go to pay his airport tax.

Now the good news is that at Heathrow, unlike many airports I could name, passengers don't pay any taxes. But just as the Information Assistant begins to say so, she is assailed by a tremendous itch and tugs at her earlobe.

Astonishing though it may seem, this simple gesture means five different things in five different Mediterranean countries.

**In America
this means 'A-OK.'**   **In France
it means 'zero.'**

Depending on his nationality, the Assistant has offered the passenger the following insult:

TO A SPANIARD: 'You rotten sponger.'
TO A GREEK: 'You'd better watch it, mate.'
TO A MALTESE: 'You're a sneaky little so-and-so.'
TO AN ITALIAN: 'Get lost you pansy.'

Only a Portuguese (to whom the gesture signifies something ineffably wonderful) would hang around long enough to hear the answer.

Happily, I can report that BAA's information staff are trained in body language.

A Sardinian woman asks if it is easy to find a taxi at Heathrow. The answer she gets is a cheery British thumbs up. (Very likely from one of the 900 cabbies who serve the airport on an average day.) Immediately, she clonks the unfortunate man with her handbag for making such a devastatingly obscene suggestion. This is why, incidentally, it's inadvisable to hitch-hike in Sardinia.

Isn't there at least one truly international gesture? Don't bet on it.

A Japanese asks an American passenger whether Heathrow has a luggage trolley service. It has. And as it happens, this service is not only first class, but FREE! So the Yank replies with the famous 'A-OK' ring gesture. But to the Japanese this signifies 'money' and he concludes there is a large charge for the service.

Meanwhile, a Tunisian on-looker thinks the American is telling the Japanese that he is a worthless rogue and he is going to kill him.

The ring-gesture can have further meanings.

A Frenchman has just read a BAA advertisement. Glancing around the restaurant in Terminal 4, he remarks wonderingly to his wife, 'You know how much zis aeroport cost the British taxpayer? Not a sou.' And he makes the finger and thumb ring which to him means 'zero.'

**At all costs
avoid the
Spanish Louse
gesture.**

Unfortunately, at the time he is glancing at a Colombian who is enjoying a fine Burgundy with his steak Bearnaise. The Colombian, enraged by the deadly obscenity which he assumes is directed at him, chokes on his wine and catches at his nose with finger and thumb.

**The Punjabi Snake Tongue
means 'you're a liar.'**

This appalls a Syrian sitting opposite, who thinks the Colombian is telling him to 'go to hell.'

The Syrian is restrained with difficulty by his Greek colleague from getting up and punching the Colombian on the nose. Meanwhile the maitre d' hurries over and attempts to calm the situation with two out-thrust

**In Japan it
means 'money.'**   **In Tunisia it means
'I'll kill you.'**

palms. This of course is taken by the Greek to be a double-'moutza' and in his rage he promptly skewers the unfortunate man with his fish knife.

Of course I am exaggerating to make a point, but I do find it astonishing that Heathrow receives only 8 complaints per 100,000 passengers. Keeping the lid on this simmering rum-punch of international emotions must take every bit as much diplomatic skill as running the United Nations.

**To a Saudi this is insulting.
To a Florentine deeply flattering.**

But even if you're never treated to such a choreography of misunderstandings, the Heathrow ballet is never dull.

Eyes peeled, next time you're there.

(And if you spot anything really unusual, like the South American Goitre Sign, or the Hawaiian Missing Bottle Waggle, do write and let me know.)

B·A·A

The world's leading international airport group.

55

25 THE RANGE OF JOBS IN THE TRAVEL INDUSTRY

The tourist industry covers a wide range of different jobs. The photographs on these pages show just some of them.

QUESTIONS

1 Study the photographs and list the tourist jobs shown in them (there may be more than one in a single photograph).
2 Place your list of tourist jobs under the following headings:
   (a) Accommodation
   (b) Tourist attractions
   (c) Recreation facilities
   (d) Catering
   (e) Entertainment
   (f) Travel and tourism organisations
   (g) Transport
   Note that the same job may be placed in more than one category.
3 How are the jobs in the photographs linked? Prepare a flow diagram to show the linkages between as many of the jobs as possible. See page 59 for an example. Can you link all 9 jobs within one flow diagram?

57

COUNTER CLERK IN TRAVEL AGENT IN CROYDON
books flight to Edinburgh for the Webber family
(Mum, Dad, Mark and Daniel)

↓

AIRLINE PILOT
flies the Webbers from Gatwick to Edinburgh

↓

CAR HIRE REPRESENTATIVE AT EDINBURGH AIRPORT
Mrs Webber hires a car for their holiday

↓

RECEPTIONIST AT ROYAL HOTEL EDINBURGH
Books the Webbers in to their room

↓

?

Flow diagram linking some of the jobs in the travel industry

26 CAREER PROFILES IN THE TRAVEL INDUSTRY

Hello. My name is Nicola Warner. I am the manager of a hotel in a small market town. I am in overall charge of running the hotel; I take responsibility for staffing and also marketing. Officially, I work a 38-hour week, but the job is so varied that I often have to work much longer hours when things are busy or there's some kind of a crisis.

It is a medium-sized hotel with 88 bedrooms. We serve a range of clients, but mainly businessmen. We offer conference and meeting facilities. I have a staff force of about 40 and I delegate some of the day-to-day responsibility to two of my younger colleagues.

I'm 34 now. I passed one A level in my Sixth Form and took a BTEC HND course at college. I had some in-service training which included working part-time towards the professional qualification of the Hotel, Catering and Institutional Management Association. I've worked in three different hotels as I've made my way up the career ladder. I'm now looking for a manager's post in a larger hotel in the city.

Name:	Terry Sayers
Age:	20
Employment:	Hotel receptionist
Qualifications:	(i) Three GCSE Grades A to C (ii) City & Guilds 709 course in Hotel Reception
Job description:	I am the first person new guests meet on their arrival at the hotel. I am responsible for reservations, record keeping, ordering room service and drawing up bills. Telephone bookings and cancellations have to be taken. I operate a computer VDU at the reception desk. I have a lot of paper work to do, but I must always be prepared for interruptions from guests. The reception desk is open 24 hours a day in a big hotel, and I have to work shifts including nights and weekends.
Career aims:	First stop is to reach supervisor. Then I've got my sights set on management, but I'll need to gain additional qualifications.

I'm Melissa Redshaw. I'm 25 and I work as an air stewardess. The first thing I must say is that it isn't as glamorous a job as many people think! Long before the passengers climb aboard the aircraft I am hard at work being briefed and checking everything is ready. Have the right number of meals been delivered? Are there enough vegetarian, halal and kosher meals? Are there enough stocks of drinks and duty-free goods? Is the emergency equipment intact? When the passengers start boarding I am kept busy settling them into their places, checking that seat belts are done up and that the gangways are clear of luggage. Before we take off I have to demonstrate the emergency procedures, including wearing and inflating a life jacket.

Once the flight has begun I have to work hard and fast to serve all the passengers in time. I work as part of a team. We serve drinks and pre-cooked meals. All the dirty trays have to be collected before the duty-free goods are sold. Passengers' enquiries have to be dealt with at any time.

I started with four GCSEs. I worked in a travel agency until I was 20. The airline ran a six week full-time training course. I then started on short domestic flights and I have progressed to short-range European flights. As I become more experienced I hope to travel on long-haul flights. On the long-hauls crews are away from the UK for two or three weeks, but they have several rest days. These give a chance to explore a foreign country and stay in hotels at the airline's expense, so I'm looking forward to such promotion.

NAME:
Alan McGregor

AGE:
19

EMPLOYMENT:
Bar staff

QUALIFICATIONS:
None essential, but City & Guilds short skills scheme for bar staff is available for school leavers. Basic mathematics is useful for till work.

JOB DESCRIPTION:
I serve beer, spirits, cocktails, fresh coffee and hot food. I also clean glasses, ashtrays and tables. I have to be able to take cash and operate the till. Also have to answer the bar telephone. Probably have to come on duty an hour before opening time, working split shifts, say 10am to 3pm and 8pm to 11pm.

CAREER AIMS:
Good prospects for promotion to supervisory and management posts, or even to the tenancy of a pub.

QUESTIONS

Work in groups of five. You are all employed by a local radio station. Your job is to plan and put together a radio programme called *The many faces of the Travel Industry*. Use the information on these pages and your own knowledge and ideas.

Your programme must have:
- An opening section which sets the scene
- A narrative commentary
- Interviews
- A concluding section

Decide who will take the roles of the presenter and the four people to be interviewed: Nicola Warner, Terry Sayers, Melissa Redshaw and Alan McGregor.

Plan your programme as a group. How will you start? What are the main points which you wish to bring across to the audience about the range of jobs in the travel industry? What questions will you ask the interviewees?

When you have completed your programme plan, make a tape or video-recording of your programme.

27 APPLYING FOR A JOB IN THE TRAVEL INDUSTRY

Trainee Counter and Reservations Clerk

We have a vacancy in our Beverley, Humberside, office for an enthusiastic college or school leaver as a counter staff trainee. The successful applicant will receive full on-the-job training; later there may be the opportunity to undertake a part-time college course in order to gain ABTA sponsored qualifications.

You must be confident in dealing with the public and providing information and advice. You must be able to stay calm and friendly under pressure. You have to balance all cash and credit transactions and maintain a complex reservations file. You must be familiar and comfortable with computer keyboards. Training will be provided in the use of our computerised reservations service.

You will need five GCSEs at grades A, B or C. Possession of a City & Guilds COTAC certificate or a City & Guilds 499 in Travel Studies would be an advantage.

Promotion prospects for counter and reservations staff to branch management are good. More limited opportunities open for branch managers to gain promotion to Head Office in York.

Salary: £5 100 p.a.

Hours: Normal shop hours, including Saturdays. A weekday in lieu.

Apply, enclosing c.v. to:
Mrs. H. Clark, Walkington Travel, Market Place, Beverley, Humberside, HU9 6BV.

WALKINGTON TRAVEL PLC

Fig. A   Advertisements like this may appear in newspapers or trade magazines

Mrs Clark will probably receive a lot of letters applying for the job with Walkington Travel. Only a few of the applicants will be called for interview; most fail. Why? What makes a successful application letter?

In the end, of course, it all comes down to one person's opinion. But following a few simple steps may give you a better chance...

1 Choose the right job to apply for

There is no point in applying for a job for which you are not suited, or in which you are not really interested. But how do you know what sort of job suits you? There are many jobs in the travel industry – which is the one for you?

Before you start thinking about this, think about *yourself*. How well do you know yourself? This may seem a strange question, but try making a list of your strengths and weaknessess. These questions may help:

- Do you prefer to work alone/in a team?
- Do you prefer to work indoors/outdoors?
- Are you tolerant/impatient?
- Are you lazy/hardworking?
- Do you have many/few interests?
- Can you cope with pressure/routine work?
- Are you well organised/muddled?
- Do you like meeting people?
- Can you work to deadlines?
- Have you any work experience?
- Are you concerned about world issues?
- Do you know much about jobs in the travel industry?

Be honest with yourself when making your lists. Don't deceive yourself about your weaknesses but don't be too modest about your strengths either! Make sure that you recognise your strengths. For example, you may have a Saturday job stocking shelves in a supermarket. Not a particularly useful job for the travel industry, you might think. However, stacking shelves requires skills of organisation and design, plus the ability to carry out instructions precisely. It means coping with a variety of goods and being prepared to carry out repetitive tasks. There may be even more there. Have you ever been asked to introduce a new employee to the job? This shows qualities of leadership and training skills, plus the fact that the employer places responsibility on you and considers you to be a reliable person.

Now that you know more about your strengths and weaknesses you will have a better idea about what kind of job will suit you. You should send for details of jobs from employers. Alternatively you could use *The Handbook of Tourism and Leisure* published annually by CRAC for the English Tourist Board. This contains detailed descriptions of many jobs in tourism and leisure. When you have seen a few jobs which interest you, try to discover what sort of person the employer is looking for. Start by finding out the answers to the following set of questions:

- What does the job involve?
- What qualifications do they seek?
- What qualities and skills are needed?
- What experience are they looking for?
- Is a certain age range specified?
- What are the career prospects?
- What is the salary?
- Where is the job located?

When you have answered those questions you must answer two further questions:

- Do you have the qualities which the employer is seeking?
- Do you want to work in that type of job?
  If the answer to both these questions is 'Yes', apply for the job.

2 Applying by telephone

Sometimes a job advertisement will ask you to telephone for further details. Follow these simple guidelines:

- Telephone from a quiet place.
- If you use a public telephone, make sure that you have more than enough money.
- Remember to take the job advertisement with you. Have a list of the points you need to cover.
- When you make the call, say clearly who you are and the job you are interested in.
- Ask for the person whose name appears on the advertisement. If there is no name, ask for the Personnel Department.
- Have pen and paper with you to write down the details of the job. Make sure that you get all the details you want.

3 Applying by letter

Most job advertisements ask you to send a letter of application. You may need to fill in an application form as well. It is better to write your letter specifically for the job, rather than to photocopy countless numbers of a general letter.

If the employer has mentioned particular qualities and skills, make sure that you point out that you have them, together with any other qualities that you think would help you. Opinions vary as to whether to type or write the letter; however, I believe that if you can type then you should do so. Make sure that your letter is neat and tidy. Make sure that your spelling is correct: ask someone to check the letter for you if you are not sure.

Give brief details of yourself and attach your curriculum vitae or cv (see Unit 28). Complete the letter with 'Yours faithfully' if it begins with 'Dear Sir' or 'Dear Madam'. Use 'Yours sincerely' if you are writing to a named person.

QUESTIONS

1 List your strengths and weaknesses.
2 Study the job advertisement in Fig A. Answer the following questions:
  (a) What does the job involve?
  (b) What qualifications do they seek?
  (c) What qualities and skills are needed?
  (d) What experience are they looking for?
  (e) Is a certain age range specified?
  (f) What are the career prospects?
  (g) What is the salary?
  (h) Where is the job located?
3 Study the application letter (Fig B) written for the job described in Fig A.
  (a) What are the strengths and weaknesses of the letter?
  (b) How can the letter be improved?
  (c) Write a letter applying for the job yourself.

1 Chepstow Close
Cottingham
Humberside

2nd July

Dear Sir

I have read your advertisement in the 'Humberside Echo' for a Counter Staff trainee. I wish to apply for that post. I enclose my cv. I feel that I have the qualifications which you seek.

I have six GCSEs at grades B and C and I have just completed a course at the Humberside College of Further Education which leads to a City & Guilds certificate. During the course I completed two week's work experience at Buttery Holidays in Beverley. The employer's report stated that I was "an enthusiastic and hardworking young woman" and concluded that "she would be a most suitable employee".

I have had a saturday job at Woolworth's for eighteen months, working on the till and general assistant duties. This has given me experience in working with the public, and of dealing with cash and credit transactions. It can get very busy in the store and I have had to work under pressure. I have found that I can remain calm and even quite enjoy the pressure.

I'd really enjoy working for you. I've been interested in the travel industry for some time. I would like the chance to be trained and to gain promotion within your company.

Yours sincerely

Sue Butterworth.

Sue Butterworth

Fig.B

28 YOUR CURRICULUM VITAE

A curriculum vitae (usually called a 'CV') is an important part of your job application. It lists essential information about yourself. Once you have drawn up a good CV you will be able to go on using it for many years, adding to it and revising it as the years go by. Your CV should be typed on one side of A4 paper. Fig A shows what you should include.

QUESTION

Type your own curriculum vitae, following the advice given in this unit.

Personal information
Here you should include:
- your full name
- date of birth and present age
- address and telephone number
- marital status (ie are you single/engaged/married?)

Employment history
Here you should include:
- all jobs, in chronological order, including part-time with dates
- details of responsibilities held
- reasons for leaving

Personal information
Name:	NEIL ANTHONY
Date of birth:	26/5/74
Age:	16 years
Address:	"Westward", Newton Road, Walkington, Lincolnshire
Telephone:	(0488) 582717
Marital status:	Single

Education and training
1985 – 1987	Kingsdown School, Swindon, Wiltshire
1987 – 1989	East Wold Upper School, Walkington, Lincolnshire (member of School Council, member of school football team)
1989 – 1990	Philip Larkin Sixth Form College, Hull
Examinations:	June 1990 (GCSE) : English Language (Grade B), English Literature (C), Mathematics (C), Biology (C), History (D), French (D), Geography (D), Design Realisation (E).
	June 1991 (GCSE): Design Realisation, French, Geography, History, Archaeology (to be taken)

Employment history:
1987 – 88	Newspaper delivery, Walkington Newsagents
1988 – present	Shop assistant, Alpha Supermarkets, Newton. In addition to stocking shelves I served on the check-outs, operating tills. I have been given the responsibility of training new employees in shelf stocking.

Interests:
Photography (I have an old Pentax SLR and I develop my own black & white prints); archaeology (I have participated in the Roman Palace dig at York); reading (I enjoy science fiction, especially Arthur C. Clarke and Isaac Asimov). I play football each weekend for a local club.

Referees:
1 Mrs A Gwinnell
   Principal
   Philip Larkin Sixth Form College
   Peppermill Road
   Hull
   HU7 6XY
   Tel: 0989 765431

2 Dr Hilary Crossley
   Manor House Surgery
   Lex Hill Road
   Newton
   Lincolnshire
   Tel: 0654 91276

Education and training
Here you should include:
- schools attended from the age of 11 (with dates)
- examinations passed with grades and dates (GCSE, A level, AS level, RSA, City & Guilds, CPVE, Highers)
- any school/college offices held
- any school/college teams of which you are/were a member
- university, polytechnic or college of Higher Education attended with dates
- degree or other qualifications gained (HND, BTEC etc)
- any offices/teams

Interests
Here you should include:
- your major interests (not just, for example, 'watching TV' or 'reading', but a description of what sort of programmes or books you enjoy)
- any achievements outside school or work, for example community activities, committees, clubs.

Fig. A

Referees
Here you should name one or two people who are prepared to write you a reference. They should vouch for your general honesty and reliability. If they are able to confirm that you possess the qualities and skills which an employer is looking for, so much the better. If you are working you should include your current employer, if you are still at school or college you should include your Headteacher or Principal. The other referee should be a person whose opinion your possible employer would respect: a teacher or a doctor, for example, *not* a member of your family.

29 INTERVIEW SKILLS

Fig. A   An interview in progress

1 Before the interview
Your application letter has earned you an interview. What now? There are several things to do before you go for the interview:

- Find out as much as you can about the company. Read again any material which the company sent you.

- Consider your answers to some of the more obvious questions which you will be asked, such as 'Why do you want this job?', 'What can you offer the company?'

- Sort out what you will wear. This will depend on the job, of course, but the basic rules are to be clean, tidy and comfortable. It is best to be smart and conventional; a suit for boys, a dress or skirt for girls.

- Ensure that you know exactly where the interview is being held. Work out how long the journey will take you and allow some extra time: it is far better to be early than to be late!

2 Going for the interview
Aim to arrive about 15 minutes before your interview appointment. Use this time to relax a little and to take in your surroundings. If your interview is being held in the building where the job will be based, what is it like? Can you see yourself working there? What are the people in the building like? They may be your colleagues: can you work with them?

Research suggests that most of us form an opinion of another person within about 90 seconds of meeting them. Think about your friends. What did you think of them when you first met? Did you instantly like them, or were your first impressions less favourable? In most aspects of life we have plenty of time to change our initial opinions of people, but this is not the case in an interview. If the first impressions you give are unfavourable and negative, you will not have time to correct them. It is vital that you make a good first impression.

You SHOULD:
- Shake the interviewer's hand
- Make eye contact and smile
- Stand up until you are invited to sit down
- Sit upright in the chair – do not slouch!
- Speak clearly, and loud enough to be heard

You should NOT:
- Sit with your arms crossed tightly in front of you
- Sit with your hands in your pockets
- Smoke
- Talk too much

Some typical interview questions
- How would you describe your home background?
- What subjects did you enjoy most at school/college? Why?
- What choices did you have at GCSE/Highers/A level?
- Which subjects did you choose?
- Why did you choose these subjects?
- What else did you do at school/college apart from your examination subjects?
- What do you do in your spare time?
- Have you had any spare-time jobs?
- What do you read?
- Which newspaper do you read?
- How would you describe your friends?
- Where have you been on holiday?
- Tell me about your most recent holiday.
- Why do you want to work for this company?
- Why have you applied for this job?
- What are your strengths and weaknesses?
- Are you an ambitious person?
- What do you want to be doing in five years time?
- Why should I employ you?

Be positive in all your answers. Do not go into too much detail about your weaknesses. But do not say that you have none. Use a weakness that can also be a strength, such as 'I am told that I get very involved with my work'. Never forget that you are trying to sell yourself. Try to direct the conversation so that it will bring out anything which you particularly want to say about yourself. Be yourself; if you are quite shy, do not pretend that you are very outgoing: it will not look convincing.

At the end of the interview you may well be asked if you have any questions to ask. The safest thing to say is, 'All my questions have already been answered', unless you have a genuine question. If you do, make sure that it is not the sort of question to which you should already know the answer.

At the end of the interview you should make a smooth exit. Thank the interviewer and shake his or her hand if it is offered.

Fig. B   Don't forget to thank the interviewer as you say goodbye

3 After the interview
When you get home, go over what occurred. In what areas did you perform well? How could you have done better? Every interview is useful practice. If you are rejected, do not take it too personally. A lot of people probably applied for the job. It is a good idea to telephone or write to the interviewer to ask why you were rejected. Say that you are not criticising the decision, but that you would appreciate advice on how to do better next time. This is not easy to do, but it may be well worth the effort.

QUESTIONS
1 Name four things which you should do before attending an interview.
2 What should you wear to an interview?
3 Answer the questions listed under the heading 'Some typical interview questions'.
4 Try to arrange a mock interview with your form tutor or another teacher. Ask if you can have the interview recorded on video or tape. Run through the interview afterwards and see where you did well and where there is room for improvement.

30 WORK EXPERIENCE

It is likely that you will be sent on one or more work experience placements during your course. Work experience is very important – in some ways, it is the most valuable part of your course. This is a great opportunity for you to find out what working in the travel industry is really like. It may help you discover whether you really want to work in this area. Sometimes work experience can be disappointing. In order to make the most of your time, you should remember the following points:

1 If you cannot go to work for any reason you MUST telephone your employer.

2 If you have any problems while at work, discuss them with someone there. If this is difficult contact your tutor or Year Head at school/college. Don't simply walk out!

3 If you are not sure what your duties are then ASK. Nobody minds helping you if you are positive and sensible.

4 Make yourself useful. If you have finished a job, don't just stand around, ask what you should do next.

During your work experience you should keep a daily diary and at the end of your time with the company you should complete a review sheet. Figs A and B show examples of the daily diary and review sheet, and give an idea of the sort of things which you could note down.

On your return to the classroom, each student in the class should prepare a ten-minute talk for the rest of the group. In your talk, stress the range of skills and environments which you encountered.

Finally, write a letter to the work experience employer which describes, explains and evaluates your experience, as well as thanking him or her for providing the experience.

THURS   DAY 24 / 2 / 91   Time of arrival: 08.30

MORNING: I sat with Kathy on the computerised reservations station. She showed me how to enter customer details onto the computer. I entered details of several holidays, including one to Papua New Guinea. The computerised reservations are very quick and efficient. At 1030 Peter asked me to join him at the counter. I spent two hours here and after a few minutes Peter asked me to greet new customers and write down their details. I enjoyed this because I was dealing with people at first hand.

AFTERNOON: I continued at the counter from 1.30 until 3.00. There was a real problem with one client's tickets: they have not arrived and she is due to leave tomorrow. Peter took this case over; I would have liked to continue with it myself.

At 3.00 I re-joined Kathy at the computer and typed in some more reservations, but soon I was asked to return to the counter because so many people came into the agents'.

Finishing time: 5.30 PM   Employer's signature B. J. C. Bates

Fig. A A daily diary

STUDENT'S REVIEW OF WORK EXPERIENCE

Student's name: _Sarah Goodyear_

Place of Work Experience: _Walkington Travel, Beverley_

Dates of Work Experience: _14.2.91 — 25.2.91_

1. THE PEOPLE YOU WORKED WITH: How were they different to what you expected?

They were friendlier and less serious than I expected — but very professional.

2. THE WORK: Describe something you learned to do; try to describe it clearly enough for one of your friends to be able to do it.

I learned to enter reservations on a computer. You follow the instructions on the V.D.U and type very carefully. You must be sure to type the details from the card in the right order. Be sure that you transmit at the end.

3. THE PLACE YOU WORKED: Describe the room or work area you felt most comfortable in, and say why.

I felt happiest when I was working on the counter. This is because I enjoyed working with members of the public rather than with a computer — but I quite enjoyed that too.

4. YOUR FEELINGS: How did you feel on Monday morning? What were the differences on Friday afternoon?

I was really nervous at first, but the staff made me very welcome. By Friday afternoon, I was really tired and looking forward to the weekend.

5. COMPARISONS: Describe three ways in which your week was either better or worse than a week in school/college (say which and why).

Better: I had real responsibility. I was doing something practical.

Worse: I had to work very hard without much of a break.

6. CONCLUSION: Tick which was most true of your week:

EXCELLENT	GOOD	SATISFACTORY	DISAPPOINTING	A DISASTER
✓	☐	☐	☐	☐

Fig. B   Student's review of work experience form

31 TECHNOLOGY IN TRAVEL AND TOURISM

A jet airliner lands in Alicante just as another takes off in Naples. Coachloads of tourists travel the roads of Europe. Ferries come and go. Trains arrive and depart, taking travellers to their holiday destinations and home again. At the height of the summer season, millions of people are on the move. How does it all work?

The modern tourist industry depends on a complex communications network, and on the ability to store and process a vast range of information. All this data must be available at the touch of a button. The modern tourist industry depends on *information technology (IT)*.

The travel agent's reservations staff are responsible for making reservations, or bookings, for all kinds of services: hotels, flights, theatre tickets, hire cars, canal boats... Most reservations staff use visual display units (VDUs) (Fig A). They can call up information about flights, check-in times, departure dates, hotel availability and so on. There may also be computerised ticket–issuing for airlines and ferry companies.

There are a number of competing systems, but *Galileo*, established in 1989, is the most important in the UK. Galileo is owned by a group of major European airlines including British Airways, Aer Lingus and Alitalia. Its headquarters and computer centre is at Swindon in Wiltshire. From here it is linked to travel agents, ticket agencies and airlines throughout Western Europe. Using 12 mainframe computers, Galileo can carry out over a thousand separate transactions *per second*.

Galileo has signed contracts with 150 of the world's 700 airlines. Their flight information is collected and displayed on a database. This gives travel agents access on one screen to information about all the flights of the participating airlines, along with details of other services, ranging from hotels to ski hire. Galileo rents and sells its computer terminals, and charges the participants (airlines, hotels and car hire companies) each time a booking is made. *Prestel* and other viewdata services are also available.

When customers decide on a flight, the computerised reservations system means that it can be booked and the ticket printed on the spot. In addition a flight can be searched for using a number of criteria: which flight arrives closest to a certain time, which is the quickest, which is the cheapest etc.

The use of video and holograms

Video recordings are used at many tourist attractions. They can provide a useful introduction to the attraction, for example by showing a re-creation of a historic site, with actors in period costume. However, in some cases video recordings may not give a clear or accurate impression. They serve as an easy way of controlling tourists and passing on information, but they lack the personal touch of a human guide, nor do recordings have the facility to answer a question.

A recent development is the use of holograms. These are three-dimensional light images of objects. They can provide highly effective exhibits. An example is the *Treasure Trapped in Light* exhibition of holograms from the Museum of Kiev in the USSR. Archaeological and art treasures, too precious and fragile to travel, have been reproduced in the form of holograms and taken on tour through Western Europe.

Fig. A   A travel agent's reservation clerk making hotel and flight reservations using a VDU

Fig. B Viking 'craftsmen' at the Jorvik Viking Centre, York

Technology at Jorvik Viking Centre

The Jorvik Viking Centre in York has become one of Britain's most popular museums. It is a new kind of museum, built on the site of the Viking city of York. A specially designed 'time car' takes visitors on a journey through Jorvik, the name by which the Vikings knew York. The Centre is a reconstruction of life in the Viking city, the result of over five years of painstaking archaeological excavation. The time cars are electrically powered and remote controlled. They hold four people. A cassette commentary is provided as the time car carries its passengers back through time, past life-size models of people from the thousand years which separate Jorvik from today (Fig B).

The technology allows the noises and the smells (both pleasant and unpleasant!) of Viking York to be experienced. The passengers on the time cars hear voices talking in Old Norse, the Viking language. By the careful use of technology, the Jorvik Viking Centre allows visitors to experience at first hand life as it once was, without the need for barriers or 'Keep off' signs. After the time car journey, visitors can walk through a display of the actual finds and then visit a shop selling souvenirs, craftwork and books.

The Jorvik Viking Centre also has a hologram of a spectacular iron and brass Anglo-Saxon helmet discovered during the excavations. The actual helmet is displayed at the Castle Museum. The hologram allows visitors to appreciate the helmet much more fully than a simple photograph would.

QUESTIONS

1 What do the letters IT stand for?
2 What are VDUs and what do many reservations staff now use them for?
3 What is Galileo?
4 Discuss the advantages and disadvantages of using video recordings at tourist sites.
5 (a) What are holograms?
   (b) What are the possible advantages of holograms?
6 How has technology been used at the Jorvik Viking Centre?
7 Make a list of other uses of technology in the travel and tourism industry. Think about credit cards, travellers' cheques, baggage handling etc.

32 THE TECHNOLOGY OF THE JET AIRLINER

The Lockheed Super Constellation was the latest thing in airliners in the mid-1950s (Fig A). It had four propellors powered by piston engines, and could cruise at 500 km per hour. The Super Constellation flew the world's main air routes. Yet within four years of its first flight, the airliner had become a museum piece. The introduction of jet-powered airliners such as the Boeing 707 (Fig B) had a dramatic effect on air transport, and upon the international tourist industry.

The new jetliners had many advantages over the piston-engined airliners:

- Jets flew faster (Boeing 707 cruising speed 920 km/h).
- Jets flew higher, taking them above the weather which made many piston-engined flights a misery for the passengers.
- Jets were much quieter (for their passengers, anyway).
- Jets were much smoother.
- Jets carried more passengers (the 707 carried 189 passengers compared with the Super Constellation's 95).

The really big advantage was speed. This allowed jets to fly twice as many flights per day as the piston-engined airliners. Twice as many flights, each carrying twice as many people, meant four times as much income for the airlines. It also enabled them to offer lower fares. In the mid-1960s several charter airlines bought jets. These jets were available for hire (charter) by holiday companies. BAC One-Elevens and Boeing 737s brought the Mediterranean resorts within two hours travelling of Gatwick, Luton and Southend airports. They could make three, or even four, return trips a day. The next decade saw a boom in inclusive tours or 'package deals', in which holiday companies offered tourists holiday rooms and flights in one all-inclusive package.

Any technological change has knock-on effects. The introduction of new jets was no exception. The new airliners were very expensive. They required much longer runways than piston-engined aircraft. Increased passenger loads meant that new, larger airport terminal buildings were needed. Airports had to be redesigned to cope with jet airliners. The surface transport systems serving the airports had to be improved as well. Technological change is interdependent – a development in one area (jet airliners) encouraged development in other areas (improved road and rail links to the airports).

For people living near the airports, the introduction of jets brought noise, smell and smoke. There were storms of protest. Plans to build new airports in southern England met fierce opposition.

Fig. A   The Lockheed Super Constellation

Fig. B   The Boeing 707

The Airbus A300 is built by Airbus Industrie, a multi-national consortium funded by French, German, British, Dutch and Spanish companies. The A300 carries up to 269 passengers in its wide-bodied fuselage. Its turbofan engines produce 23 000 kg of thrust which allow the Airbus to cruise at over 900 km/hr. More than 320 A300s are operated by 50 airlines throughout the world.

Fig. C   The Airbus A300

QUESTIONS

1 Draw up two lists, one showing the advantages and the second the disadvantages of the introduction of jet airliners.
2 Why did the introduction of jet airliners provide the basis for the Inclusive Tour boom of the 1960s?
3 Fig D gives performance statistics for a typical airliner of the 1950s and 1990s. These airliners flew tourists on inclusive tour flights.
   (a) Calculate the time taken for each aircraft to fly from London (Gatwick) to Palma, Majorca, a distance of 1200 km, at cruising speed.
   (b) Calculate the time required for a return flight from Gatwick to Palma for each airliner. Do not forget to include the turn-round time.
   (c) If the airliners flew a continual shuttle service, with minimum turn-round time, how many flights could they operate in 24 hours?

	Douglas DC-4 (1950s)	Airbus A300 (1990s)
Cruising speed (km/hr):	400	900
Range (km):	4025	6000
Service ceiling (m):	6800	11000
Passengers:	86	269
Turn-round time (mins):	50	30

Fig. D   Performance statistics for a typical airliner of the 1950s and 1990s

33 THE CHANNEL TUNNEL AND THE TGV

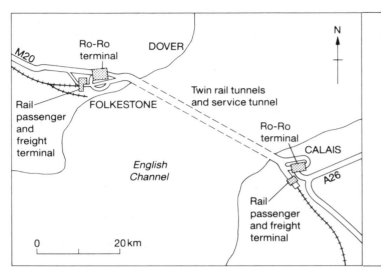

Fig. A   The Channel Tunnel

CHANNEL TUNNEL STATISTICS	
Length	49.4 km (38.0 km undersea)
Depth	25-40 m below seabed (maximum 100 m below sea level)
Internal diameters	7.6 m rail tunnels; 4.8 m service tunnel
Shuttle train capacity	185 cars on passenger trains; 25 lorries on freight trains
Journey time	30 minutes; shuttles at 5 minute intervals at peak times

In 1993 Britain will no longer be an island. The Channel Tunnel will link it with the mainland of Europe. This simple geographical fact will have important repercussions for the travel industry.

1 The owners of the Tunnel estimate that they will carry over 40% of cross-Channel passengers.
2 Up to 6600 jobs will be lost by the cross-Channel ferry operators, others in airlines will be at risk.
3 Up to 5000 people will be employed to staff the tunnel.
4 Thousands of other jobs will be created, in engineering, transport and, not least, in tourism.

Fig. B   An artist's impression of the shuttle trains which will use the Tunnel

When the Tunnel is open it will bring over 50 million people on the continent of Europe within four hours travelling time of Kent and 30 million Britons within four hours of the continent. Kent is already an important centre for tourism. The vastly increased hinterland will place more pressure on already popular attractions such as Canterbury Cathedral and Leeds Castle. With the cross-Channel journey time reduced to just 30 minutes, cross-Channel day-trips will become much more popular.

These new opportunities for tourism are closely connected with recent technological developments in railways. In 1981 France launched its TGV (Train à Grande Vitesse – High Speed Train) into service between Paris and Lyons on a brand-new railway line (Fig C). TGV travels at speeds of up to 275 km per hour. The journey time from Paris to Lyons was cut from four hours to just two. The introduction had a dramatic effect on passenger numbers too: within four years numbers had doubled to 24 million per year. The major loser in TGV's success has been the airlines. Air Inter's traffic between Paris and Lyons was halved following the introduction of TGV on the route. A new TGV-Atlantique route opened between Paris and Le Mans and Tours in 1989 (Fig D), and will be extended to Nantes and Bordeaux.

Plans to build a new high-speed railway between London and the Tunnel caused uproar in the Kent villages along the proposed route. The noise and extra traffic which the Tunnel will bring threatens the Kent countryside. Plans to build many warehouses and industrial units will add to the demands on land

Fig.C TGV

in Kent. These are some of the costs of the Channel Tunnel. Any new development will bring both costs and benefits; it is the balance between them which has to be carefully considered. A person's opinion of the Channel Tunnel depends on how they will be affected. For some it offers the prospect of quicker, more efficient travel and new business opportunities. Others fear damage to the environment and their quality of life.

QUESTIONS

1 What effects may the opening of the Channel Tunnel have on the tourist industry?
2 (a) What is the TGV?
   (b) Why do you think that a new railway line had to be built for the TGV?
3 What evidence is there that the TGV has been successful?
4 Study Fig E and state the travelling times before and after the introduction of TGV on the following routes: (i) Paris – Lyons (ii) Paris – Bordeaux (iii) Lyons – Marseilles.
5 Copy Fig D and extend the Paris – Nantes line to Brest (before TGV 6 hours; with TGV 4 hours).
6 Fig E shows the time taken to fly from London to Paris. Draw a similar divided bar to show the time taken to travel between London and Paris via the Channel Tunnel. Use the following journey details and times:

Walk from central London office to tube station	10
Tube trip to London tunnel terminal	15
Check in and await train	30
Journey time	190
Metro to central Paris	20

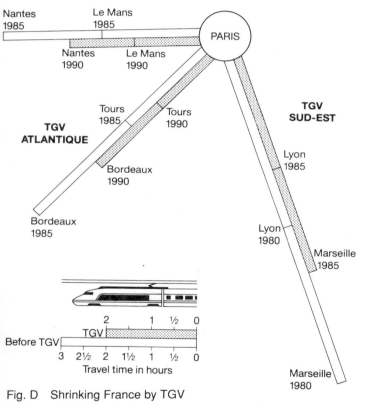

Fig. D Shrinking France by TGV

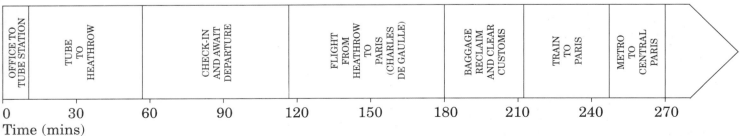

Time (mins)

Fig.E Time taken to travel from London to Paris via airline

34 TOURIST IMAGE CAMPAIGNS

An important part of the promotion of a tourist area is the *image* which is conveyed to potential travellers. How do travel companies convey image? How do the images vary for different types of customer?

Advertising is the means of conveying the image. Travel advertisements may appear on television, in magazines and newspapers, on posters and hoardings. Whatever the form, the advertisement must present a powerful image in a very limited space or time. It has to interest you in a particular holiday destination, and persuade you that you want to go there.

Fig. A

Fig. B

QUESTIONS

1 Look at the examples in Figs A and B.
  (a) What image are the two advertisements trying to convey? Think about the words used to describe the places and give examples of phrases which convey the image.
  (b) What do the drawings in each advertisement show? How do these help to convey the image?
2 Study Fig C.
  (a) How does this advertisement differ from those in Figs A and B?
  (b) What image of the company's holidays is this advertisement trying to convey?

Fig. C

Advertisements often advise customers to consult a travel agent or to write or telephone for a brochure. The *brochure* is the key to a successful tourist image campaign (Fig D).

3 Obtain copies of travel brochures and advertisements from travel agents, newspapers, magazines, national tourist offices and embassies, holiday companies.

Try to obtain the following companies' brochures: Intasun, SunMed, Kuoni Worldwide, Thomsons.

(a) Study the advertisements which you have obtained. Write a brief description of the *style* of each. Then do the same for the brochures.

(b) Choose four destinations. Make a copy of the table below and complete it for the four destinations. In the third column write your own ideas about how the country might have problems in maintaining the tourist image. An example has been done for you.

Tourist destination	Images conveyed	Possible problems
Kenya	Wildlife	Need to preserve animals and their habitats but also allow tourists to see them.
	Traditional crafts	Have to make enough to sell to tourists, but need to keep 'traditional' skills.

(c) Choose four destinations which are featured in at least two of the brochures. Compare the way the brochures promote the same destination. What similarities and differences are there in their approaches?

4 Tourist brochures want to sell a product. They may ignore or gloss over the problems of a destination. The Kuoni Worldwide brochure does not do this. Form a group of three or four and read the extract (Fig E). Then discuss the following questions:

(a) How does the extract's presentation of the Caribbean as a holiday destination differ from those in the brochures you have looked at?

(b) What reasons might Kuoni have for using a different approach?

5 Imagine you work for a travel company which wishes to promote the place where you live as a new holiday destination. Create a brochure for your area. Write a description and include a map, sketches and photographs if possible.

Fig. D   Tourist brochures convey an image of the sorts of holiday they offer

'A holiday in the Caribbean is for many a life-long dream – but unless you know which island suits your mood and which hotel out of the vast range is to your taste, it may well be a shattered one. If in doubt please do ask one of our experts. Food and beverages throughout the Caribbean are generally more expensive than at home but fortunately measures for drinks are generous. There are exceptions, but in general food throughout the Caribbean is not as good or exotic as you might have imagined from the posters and advertisements which beckon you to these islands. Most food is imported, foreign wines are expensive and service leisurely'

Fig. E   From the Kuoni *Worldwide* Brochure

35 PRODUCING A TOURIST DESIGN

The aim of this unit is to provide you with information as the basis for a design folder.

Tourist designs work within certain limits. The most important is the *target audience*. What image does the design hope to convey? What colours/shades are most suitable for the market aimed at? In the case of an airline, should the design of the aircraft colour scheme be modern and trendy, or restrained and conservative? Different colours have different effects. For example, red is often associated with anger, or with speed; blue is a calm, but cool, colour.

To answer these questions the designers need to know who the airline's passengers are and what they want from the airline. Do they want an exciting,

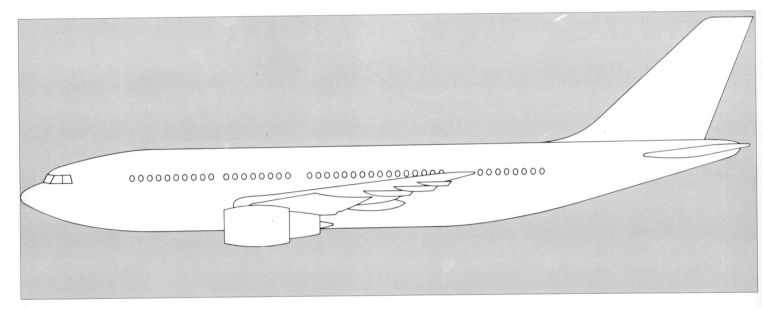

Fig. A   The A310 airliner

MEMORANDUM

FROM: EXEC
TO: Design Team
DATE: Tuesday 17 August

For the launch next month (Friday 21st) we'll need detailed plans and designs for:

i   Company Logo and colour scheme

ii   Uniform to be worn by representatives and aircrew

iii   Airline colour scheme for NEW HORIZON AIR's A310s.

As you know, the company wishes to portray a crisp, clean, efficient image. The designs should be stylish but not over-elaborate. Simplicity should be coupled with distinctiveness. We want to appeal to both holidaymakers and business people.

You have ten days to produce preliminary versions of the above. Submit to Exec. by 0930 Friday 27th.

Make it good.

MJP

Fig. B

CONSFIN to authorised Newsagencies and broadcast agencies

DATE: 19.9

PRESS RELEASE: MAJOR NEW TRAVEL COMPANY ESTABLISHED

(NOT for publication or broadcast before 0900 Friday 21st)

DETAIL:

Long-established UK finance house Consolidated Finance plc announces the establishment of a major new travel company. Named NEW HORIZON TRAVEL, the company will concentrate on inclusive tour package holidays to resorts in the Mediterranean area, Madeira and the Canary Islands, with later planned expansion to include more long-distance destinations such as Florida and the Far East. Publicity will be through travel agents and direct selling to the public. NEW HORIZON has negotiated an agreement with Pluto Holidays plc which will give full access to Pluto's chain of travel agents and computer network.

NEW HORIZON will own an associated company, NEW HORIZON AIR, which will operate three Airbus A310 airliners. Seat capacity will be reserved on other airlines as and when appropriate. NEW HORIZON AIR will be based at London (Stansted) Airport and will also operate from Manchester, Birmingham and Bournemouth (Hurn) airports. If expansion proceeds as scheduled, NEW HORIZON AIR will lease further A310 airliners and seek ATLB licences to operate scheduled services between London (Stansted) and Palma, Malaga, Tenerife and Athens.

NEW HORIZON will initially employ a staff of 600. Headquarters will be at Canary Wharf, London. Branch offices will be at Peterborough and Stockport.

Details of company logo, uniform and colour scheme to be released Friday 28th.

Fig. C Press release

high-tech image, or would they prefer something more conventional? Which design gives the strongest impression of safety and efficiency, for example? Which design conveys fun and enjoyment? Other limiting factors include cost, safety and the laws of copyright.

QUESTIONS

New Horizon Travel is a major new travel company established by a leading finance company.

You work in the Design Team of New Horizon Travel. A memo (Fig B) and a Press Release (Fig C) have just landed on your desk. You must carry out the instructions in the memo. Choose the logo, the airline colour scheme, or the uniform. Prepare designs for your chosen subject. If you choose the airline colour scheme, make a copy of the airliner outline provided for you (Fig A) to display your design. Present your design on plain A4 paper and store it in a design folder. You can provide up to three alternative designs with your folder.

Perhaps you could conduct a survey of students in your school/college, to find out which design is most popular, and why.

36 A SURVEY OF LEISURE TIME ACTIVITIES

How do people spend their leisure time? The Government's annual publication *Social Trends* contains the results of sample surveys of people's leisure activities. Your school or college library may have this publication. If not, your central town library certainly will. Fig A shows information taken from some surveys in *Social Trends*.

The sample survey covers nearly 20 000 people. Design a similar questionnaire to discover the leisure activities of people in your area. Here are the steps to follow:

1 The aims
First of all, decide what your survey is aiming to find out. You could choose a simple aim such as finding out how your local area compares with the national picture. You can express your aim as a question to be answered, or as a *hypothesis* to be tested:

Question: 'How do the leisure activities of people in my local area compare with the national average as given in *Social Trends*'?

Hypothesis: 'The leisure activities of people in my local area are the same as the national average.'

However, you could decide on a more complex series of aims. For example, you could see if there was any pattern to the leisure activities which people of different age groups participate in. The statistics in *Social Trends* are divided into the following age-groups: 16–19, 20–29, 30–59, 60 and over.

2 What questions should you ask?
You could simply repeat the survey as it is printed in *Social Trends*, in which case your questions are done for you already. However, you may decide that you want to ask some extra questions.

Work in groups of three or four. Decide on some extra activities to ask about, such as 'going to a Sports Centre'. Then design your questionnaire. Do not forget to include the person's age group on the questionnaire.

3 Carrying out the survey
You can conduct your survey in one of two ways:

1 You can stop people in the street and ask them questions;

2 You can visit their homes and ask them questions.

In order to get a representative sample you need to ask a minimum of 30 people, preferably more.

Your questionnaire for this survey is likely to be long, with over 20 questions. If you use the first method, you may well find that people become impatient at the time it takes. It helps if you select people to ask who do not seem to be in a hurry (bus queues are ideal). It may well be better to ask the people at home. It is *not* a good idea to knock on people's doors and ask them the questions on their doorsteps. It is far better to push the questionnaire through their letterboxes with a note saying that you will call round in a couple of days to collect it.

Whichever method you choose, NEVER WORK ALONE.

4 Presenting the data
You have 30 or so completed questionnaires. What are you going to do with the data you have obtained?

- The first thing to do is to record the answers to all the questions on a single sheet, like Fig A. Do not forget to convert the numbers to percentages.
- You can present the data in a variety of ways. Simple pie or bar graphs are very effective (Fig B). There are computer programs available to draw such graphs for you.

5 Analysing your data
Study your results carefully. Use the questions as the basic structure of your analysis. What do the answers tell you? Which were the most popular activities? Did the accessibility of certain leisure activities (such as cinemas) affect the results?

Are the results what you expected? If not, why not?

6 Conclusions
Give an oral presentation of your study to the rest of your class. Use overhead projector transparencies of your tables and graphs. Give a summary of your study. What were the aims of your investigation? How did you go about it? What results did you obtain? Has the question posed at the outset been answered? Alternatively, do your results lead you to accept or reject your hypothesis? How could your study be improved?

QUESTIONS

1 Study the data in Fig A carefully.
   (a) Name three leisure activities more popular with males than with females.
   (b) Name three leisure activities more popular with females than with males.
   (c) What is the most popular type of destination for an open air outing?
   (d) What is the most popular entertainment, social and cultural activity?
   (e) What is the most popular home-based activity?

Percentage of people (aged 16 or over) engaging in each activity in the 4 weeks before interview:

	Male	Female
Open air outings		
Seaside	6	8
Country	3	3
Parks	3	4
Entertainment, social and cultural activities		
Going to the cinema	8	8
Visiting historic buildings	9	10
Going to the theatre/opera/ballet	4	6
Going to museums/art galleries	4	4
Amateur music/drama	4	3
Going to fairs/amusement arcades	4	5
Going out for a meal	47	47
Going out for a drink	65	47
Dancing	9	12
Home-based activites		
Listening to records/tapes	69	65
Gardening	47	39
Needlework/knitting	3	48
House repairs/DIY	54	27
Reading books	52	64

Fig. A

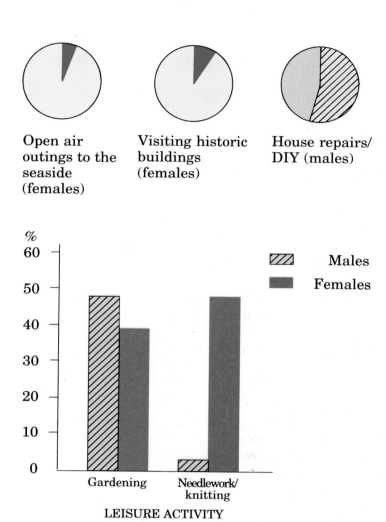

Open air outings to the seaside (females)

Visiting historic buildings (females)

House repairs/DIY (males)

Fig. B   Data obtained from the survey can be presented in a number of ways

37 SPECIAL INTEREST HOLIDAYS

What's your idea of an ideal holiday? Not everyone wants to laze on a sunny beach or lie beside a hotel swimming pool. Recently there has been a rapid growth in 'special interest' holidays as increasing numbers of tourists seek a more active holiday (Fig A). Such a holiday may be active physically, or mentally. Tourists have come to expect more from their holiday than simply a change of scene: travel is no longer the main attraction. The advertisements and photographs in this unit show just a few special interest holidays. There are many companies specialising in each interest area.

COUNTY PURSUITS

If you're interested in gardening, our nationwide network of on-the-spot contacts will take you into some of Britain's finest gardens in a Garden Appreciation break. As for Bridge-players, there are none so advanced that they don't find their pleasure of the game hugely increased by our Duplicate Bridge breaks, licensed by the English Bridge Union. The same goes for people on a Painting in Water Colours break: they find that – encouraged by ravishing countryside and expert instruction from local artists – their technique improves dramatically.

Music at Leisure's 24 years' experience is reflected in the superb flair and organisation that characterise our musical breaks. If you've ever wanted to deepen your understanding of a favourite writer or composer, our Character Trails help you do just that – with breaks centred on the landscapes that inspired and shaped their work: Jane Austen, Lord Byron, James Herriot, to name but a few.

If, like Sherlock Holmes, you're never happier than when the game's afoot, you should investigate our Murder & Mystery Breaks.

from Trusthouse Forte brochure *County Pursuits – Special Interest Breaks*

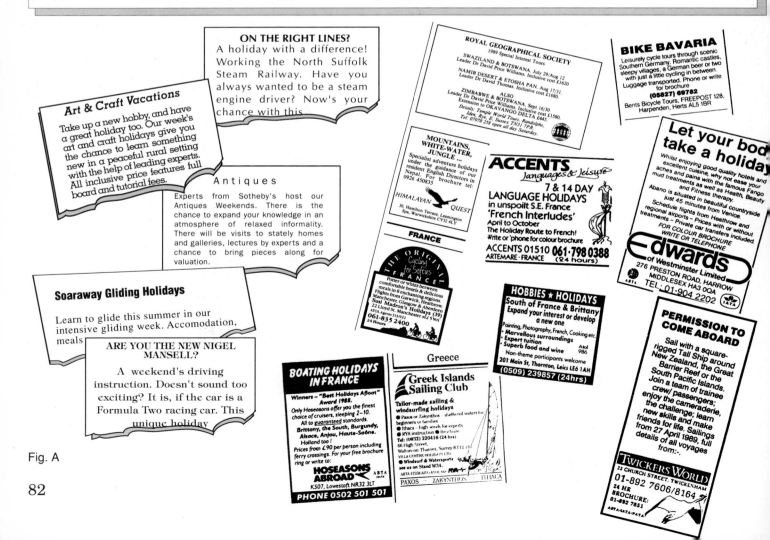

Fig. A

QUESTIONS

1 Study the advertisements for holidays (Fig A). Make two lists, one of holidays which are physically active and the other of holidays which are for those with special interests or hobbies.
2 (a) What are the attractions of special interest holidays?
  (b) Why do you think special interest holidays are increasing in popularity?
  (c) Can you think of any possible disadvantages of such holidays? (Hint: safety)

3 Plan a new idea in special interest holidays.
  (a) Think of an idea.
  (b) Decide upon the best way to organise your new holiday. Write out a programme for four days. Will you include lectures, demonstrations, visits?
  (c) Design an advertising campaign for your new holiday. This should include a small newspaper advertisement and a larger information sheet giving as much information as possible about the holiday, eg type of activity, accomodation, location...

Fig. B Special interest or activity holidays are becoming increasingly popular

38 FOOD AND TOURISM

Istanbul 4th August Having a great time. The weather is hot and sunny. The hotel is comfortable. The food is marvellous – so varied, and so beautifully presented. It certainly beats the pub food at home! And the drinks – so many amazing cocktails and liquers. You would love it! *Neil + Judy*

ROBERT CORNFORD
2 WEBBER'S CLOSE
CHESTER
ENGLAND
CR2 1OX

Fig. A   A postcard from Turkey

The weather, the accommodation, the sights – all important parts of a holiday. The food and drink available in a resort can be just as important as any of these.

Turkish cuisine, for example, is rated one of the highest in the world. For those who know only shish kebab, the quality and breadth of Turkish food comes as a revelation. A full Turkish meal would start with a glass of raki, an aperitif distilled from grape juice and flavoured with aniseed. The raki will be accompanied by a vast selection of appetizers called *meze* (Fig B). Examples are stuffed green peppers, stuffed vine leaves, chopped cucumber and yoghurt, and fried aubergine slices. Unleavened bread can be eaten with a variety of dips including fish roe mixed with lemon juice and oil, and thyme-flavoured yoghurt.

The main course is usually lamb, poultry or fish. Pork is forbidden to Moslems. There are few cattle in Turkey so beef is rare and therefore expensive. Examples of main courses include the famous shish kebab (lamb, onion and tomatoes grilled on a spit) and doner kebab (lamb and beef grilled on a vertical spit and cut off in slices). Other excellent main courses include kuzu dolmasi (grilled lamb, stuffed

with rice, raisins and pine nuts) and guvec (steamed lamb with rice, vegetables, tomatoes and paprika). Fish dishes include swordfish, bluefish, anchovies and red mullet. In many main courses olive oil, garlic and yoghurt are used.

Turkish desserts include baklava (a pastry with walnuts soaked in honey), marrow boiled with sugar and sprinkled with grated nuts, and waffles stuffed with pistachio nuts and dipped in milk. Beverages include *boza* (a sour drink made from fermented millet) and *ayran* (goat's milk yoghurt whipped with water). Turkey's climate makes it unsuitable for dairy cattle, so cow's milk is quite rare.

Great care is taken with the preparation and presentation of the food. The mezes are often placed on intricate designs of lettuce and vine leaves. Flowers and herbs decorate the dips.

Tourists from Western Europe and America find that eating out in Turkey is cheaper than at home. Many tourists are happy to eat out every day, working their way through the extensive menus. A Turkish meal takes at least an hour, probably nearer two, to eat. The atmosphere is relaxed and the food is savoured. This is in complete contrast to the 'fast food' approach to eating!

QUESTIONS

1 What are mezes?
2 Prepare a menu for a Turkish-style meal. Select and organise your food items from those given in the text. List the aperitif, mezes, main course and desserts.
3 What evidence is there in the text that the Turks value their food highly?
4 How are the following foods affected by the climate or culture of Turkey: (a) beef (b) pork (c) dairy products?
5 Read Fig D. What evidence is there in the article of climatic and environmental effects on the regional cuisine of Italy?

'When one thinks of food – good food that one remembers and wants to eat again – two countries automatically spring to mind: Italy and France... Every town, every village and even every hamlet in Italy has gastronomic specialities which are treasures in their own right and superb examples of a cuisine which, in essence, is completely unpretentious. A conservative estimate places Italy's speciality dishes at around 300 and her regional wines at a minimum of 225.

For example, Tuscany boasts grilled Florentine steaks – thick and succulent and weighing at least half a kilogram. Equally outstanding is the light and sweet olive oil, the superb breads made from locally-grown wheat, haricot broth flavoured with tomatoes and celery (Minestrone di Fagioli), mussel soup, and a delicious tripe stew cooked in a Bolognese sauce and served with clouds of Parmesan cheese.

Basilicata is a mountainous region with very few arable pastures. Thus the people depend on thick broths made from vegetables they grow themselves, barbecued and marinated eel (from Lake Monticchio), heavily-spiced sausages, and macaroni with strongly-flavoured sauces.

Calabria, next door to Basilicata, is also mountainous but marginally more fertile and, as a result, one can find excellent roast pork, trout, smoked sausages, Ricotta cheese, stuffed aubergines and macaroni with ginger-flavoured tomato sauce.'

from *European Cooking* Sonia Allison (Collins).

Fig. D   Italian cuisine

Fig. B   Turkish mezes

Fig. C   Turkish dessert

39 FOOD, HEALTH AND HYGIENE

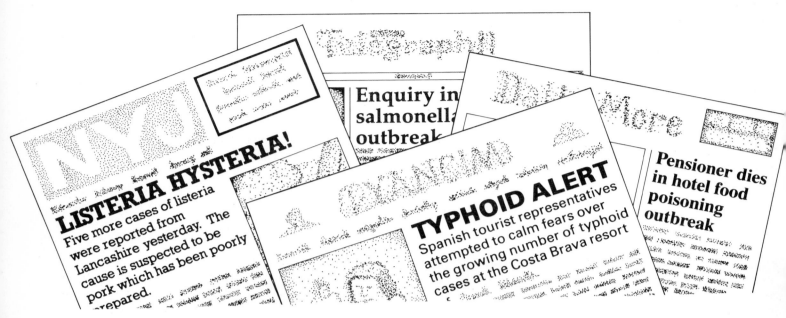

Fig. A

Strict Health and Safety regulations apply to any business that provides food for tourists. Hotels, restaurants, airlines etc must take great care over hygiene and correct temperature control. When things go wrong, the problems hit the headlines (Fig A).

Fortunately, outbreaks of food poisoning are quite rare, but *everyone* in the tourist industry must be aware of the risks and take effective precautions (Fig B).

PERSONAL HYGIENE AFFECTING FOOD PREPARATION

- There are always germs living on your skin. Failure to wash your hands before preparing food can result in the transfer of the germs to the food and illness for those unfortunate enough to eat the food.
- The germs which cause serious illness such as dysentery and typhoid are passed out of the body through the bowels. Failure to wash your hands after going to the toilet can pass the germs onto food.
- Coughing over food can pass on germs very effectively.
- Septic wounds on hands can also pass on infections.
- Keep animals away from food.

The real enemy is the canteen worker with a boil, a discharging nose, dirty hands, or a septic finger. Frankly, these infections are caused by dirty or stupid people who do not realise that their sore finger can become someone else's diarrhoea and vomiting. Those in charge of canteens or restaurants must ensure that staff is supervised, that anyone with a septic infection is put off duty, and that all know about washing after visiting the lavatory and absolute cleanliness.

Fig. B   From *Pears Cyclopaedia* (Pelham Books)

What is food poisoning? The two most common forms are salmonella and listeria infections. Salmonella bacteria live in the guts of animals and humans. They are transferred to the meat either when the slaughtered animal is gutted, or through animal feed contaminated with salmonella. 80% of food poisoning outbreaks are caused by salmonella. In 1988 there were over 45 000 reported cases, a worrying increase from the 25 000 reported in 1986. Salmonella infections affect the small intestine and cause vomiting, severe abdominal pain and diarrhoea. Such symptoms occur about one day after eating infected food and usually clear up within about ten days, but sometimes death can result, especially for the young or elderly.

Listeria is a widespread bacteria found in soil, water, on plants and in animal and human excrement. Listeriosis infection can affect people with weak or altered immune systems such as babies, the elderly and pregnant women. In 1988 there were 300 reported cases of listeriosis. The real concern about listeriosis is the link between cook-chill ready meals which, if not kept at the right temperature, can provide a breeding ground for listeria. Temperature control and proper handling are effective at controlling listeriosis (Fig C).

Tourists are especially susceptible to stomach upset or diarrhoea. This is usually caused by sensitivity to unfamiliar food and drink. In some areas water supplies are not fit for drinking. Bottled water provides a cheap alternative. Although some tourists rigorously avoid tapwater, they may become infected by ice cubes in their drinks or by eating salads which have been washed in dirty water.

QUESTIONS

1 (a) What are salmonella and listeria?
  (b) Which of the two is the most common cause of food poisoning?
  (c) What are the symptoms of salmonella infections?
  (d) What type of people are especially vulnerable to listeriosis?
2 Explain in your own words why anyone involved in food preparation must wash their hands frequently.
3 Prepare a ten minute talk on the subject of 'Avoiding food poisoning through hygiene in the kitchen'. Produce any visual aids which you may wish to use. Give your talk to the rest of your class.
4 Why should tourists beware of eating salads and having ice cubes in their drinks in certain countries?

HYGIENE IN THE KITCHEN

Chilled and frozen food contains bacteria. Most bacteria stop growing at temperatures below 5°C, but they do not die. When such foods are removed from the refrigerator or freezer the temperature rises and the bacteria reproduce every 10 to 12 minutes. This means that food contaminated with just one bacterium could contain 3 500 million within six hours!

It is essential that re-heating reaches a high temperature. Most bacteria die if they are cooked at 75°C for 12 minutes. It is vital that the food is heated right through to a minimum of 75°C. It should be served immediately while piping hot. The food should not be kept warm as food poisoning bacteria grow quickly between 10°C and 60°C. Fears have been expressed over microwave ovens, but if the manufacturer's instructions are followed to the letter, including standing time, there should be no problem.

A common way of spreading food poisoning in the kitchen is by cross contamination. In order to avoid this:

* Always keep raw and cooked meats apart.

* Knives, worksurfaces and chopping boards should be kept clean, especially where raw meat is handled.

Fig. C Strict attention to hygiene and temperature control is essential when preparing food

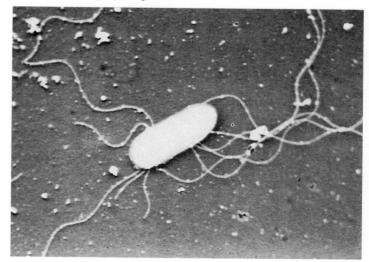

Fig. D Salmonella bacteria

40 ROLE PLAY: PLANNING A TOURIST FESTIVAL

The imaginary industrial town of Goodbury is planning a tourist festival next summer. The festival will last a week. You are a member of the Festival Planning Committee. Work with the other members to prepare plans for the festival.

QUESTIONS

1 Study the information about Goodbury (Fig A) and the map of the town (Fig B).
   (a) What is the population of Goodbury?
   (b) Why was Goodbury important in the past?
   (c) What industries grew up in Goodbury?
   (d) List the surviving evidence of Goodbury's industrial past.
   (e) How could these relics be made into tourist attractions? What sort of people would be interested in them?

2 Read the five role cards (Fig C).
   (a) Form a group of five. Each group member should be allocated a role. Read the role carefully and think about the attitudes of the person: what would they think about the festival? Now plan one aspect of your role. For example, Judy Sayers would want to consider long-term developments such as a new landscaped garden area in the Arthur Burrowes Memorial Park. Write down an outline of your plan.

   (b) Hold a meeting to discuss the plans for the festival. Each group member should present their proposals to the committee. Following the presentations the committee has to answer the following questions:
   ● What type of events could be organised?
   ● Where would they be held?
   ● What problems will you face?
   ● How is the festival to be paid for?
   ● Who will take responsibility for organising and running events?
   ● What advertising will you need?
   If you cannot reach agreement on any matter, you may hold a vote and proceed with the majority's decision.

   (c) Produce a pamphlet providing a programme of events during the week and giving information for tourists. Include a simple town map.

Today Goodbury is a small industrial town with an air of stagnation, even decay. Yet it is easy to see traces of the town's illustrious past when it was at the forefront of the Industrial Revolution. It is best to start a kilometre or so north of the town where a small privately-owned coal mine still operates on traditional lines with pit ponies and hand-held power tools, the sole survivor of over two dozen drift and shaft mines in the Goodbury area.

A small branch still links the mine with the main line of the Mid-Western Canal which runs through Goodbury. Long since abandoned by commerce, the Mid-Western Canal is still navigable for pleasure boats. The canal wharf in Goodbury stands derelict and decaying, its small Georgian warehouses still largely intact, but with broken windows and peeling paintwork. Through the wharf once passed the coal from Goodbury's mines and the iron from the town's ironworks. Nothing now remains of the former Queen Caroline ironworks, but the brick furnaces and hammer forges of the Goodbury Iron Foundry can still be seen, on the southern side of the Arthur Burrowes Memorial Park.

Perhaps the most remarkable survivor from Goodbury's early industrial days is the Iron Works Village, a small estate built to house the workers at the Goodbury Iron Foundry. These tiny, but well-built terraced stone cottages provide a fascinating insight into the home life of the ironworkers of the early 19th century. Whilst some of the cottages have been damaged by later 'improvement', several remain in a condition similar to that in which they were built.

Fig. A   A description of Goodbury from the book *Towns of the Welsh Marches* by Trevor Buttery

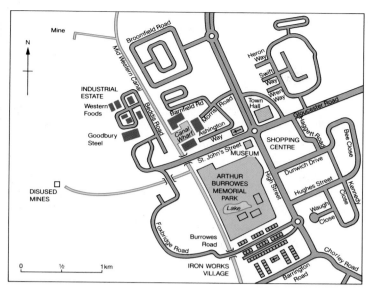

Fig. B   Map of Goodbury

JUDY SAYERS:
Goodbury District Council Senior Planning Officer

Age: 31

The District Council has agreed to provide £10 000 to support the Festival, but is keen to see others provide the rest of the money. The Council wants you to seek out ways to attract money from private companies in order to avoid the need for further council funding. The council is also keen to see developments of long-term use to Goodbury, rather than simply for the week of the festival alone.

JAN HARWOOD:
Goodbury Steel Fabrications plc

Age: 36

You represent Goodbury's second largest industrial employer, and one of the town's oldest-established firms. Your company is very keen to be associated with the festival for publicity purposes. It is happy to contribute money to the festival, but will only consider a substantial sum if the Goodbury Steel name is included in the title of the festival and on the publicity.

Inspector HELEN HOLLAND:
Goodbury Police

Age: 46

The police are concerned about traffic congestion and safety aspects of the festival. They are prepared to bring in extra police for any major events, but would prefer to keep extra policing to a minimum.

MICHAEL SNELGROVE:
Goodbury Board of Commerce

Age: 55

You represent the shopkeepers of Goodbury. You are keen for the festival to succeed in order to see increased custom for Goodbury's shops. You are prepared to contribute some money to the cost of the festival, but your organisation is not a wealthy one. You are determined to ensure that many of the festival events take place in or near the town centre where the majority of your members' shops are located.

STEPHEN GOODMAN:
Western Foods plc

Age: 23

You represent Western Foods, Goodbury's largest industrial employer. Your company is keen to be associated with the festival. The publicity would be very useful at a time when competition in the food industry is increasing. The company would be happy to contribute a substantial sum to the organisation of the festival provided that the Western Foods name is included in the title of the festival and on the publicity material.

Fig. C   Role cards

41 ASSESSMENT FOR SECTION ONE

1 (a) Give one way in which three of the following factors affect people's choice of tourist destination:
(i) climate, (ii) distance, (iii) time, (iv) perception.

(3 marks)

(b) Name two other factors and explain how they affect people's choice.

(4 marks)

2 Fig A shows the tourist 'top ten' countries.
(a) Draw a bar graph to illustrate these statistics.

(10 marks)

(b) For five of the countries, name a famous tourist resort and state its attractions for tourism.

(10 marks)

(c) Five million British tourists visit Spain each year, but only 340 000 Spanish tourists visit the UK. Explain the difference.

(6 marks)

3 (a) Identify the four National Parks shown on Fig B.

(4 marks)

(b) For each, give one attraction the Park has for tourists.

(4 marks)

(c) Name the National Park described in each of the following:
(i) Being within a short distance of the cities of Manchester and Sheffield this National Park receives a high number of visitors, many on day-trips.

(1 mark)

(ii) An area of high moorland close to the Scottish border which includes the Cheviot Hills and the Kielder Forest.

(1 mark)

(iii) Although there are no mountains, the beautiful coastline of this Welsh National Park attracts many tourists.

(1 mark)

Country	Number of tourists (millions)
Spain	43
France	37
Italy	25
USA	21
UK	15
Austria	15
Canada	13
West Germany	13
Hungary	10
Switzerland	10

Fig. A   The ten countries with most tourist visits

Fig. B

4 For one National Park which you have studied:
   (a) Name the National Park, and name one town within the Park area.

   (2 marks)

   (b) Describe the Park's attractions for tourists.

   (5 marks)

   (c) What benefits and problems are caused by the tourists who visit the Park?

   (5 marks)

5 Read the newspaper article (Fig C).
   (a) Explain the meaning of the article's title.

   (3 marks)

   (b) What evidence is there in the article to support the following statements:
   (i) 'Tourism has become a very important industry.'

   (3 marks)

   (ii) 'Tourism seems to be growing unchecked.'

   (3 marks)

   (iii) 'Regional distribution of international tourism has altered only slowly.'

   (3 marks)

   (c) What two developments does Dr Pahr insist are occurring in tourist expectations?

   (2 marks)

TOTAL: 70 marks

WHY I'D MUCH RATHER BE IN CALIFORNIA

Michael Thompson-Noel

The politicians and bureaucrats have made such a mess of the capital that I am coming to the view that it is marginally easier – or, at any rate, less stressful – to travel really long distances (California, say) than to traverse London.

Tourism seems to be growing unchecked. It is already a big industry, but will become much bigger – piling up enormous problems in the years ahead. Dr. W. Pahr, secretary-general of the World Tourism Organisation (WTO), writes 'Tourism has become a very important industry...in 1987, it generated 12% of world gross national product and accounted for over 5% of world trade. Twenty out of every hundred workers are employed in tourism-related activities. According to WTO statistics, some 355 million international tourists spent around $150 billion dollars in 1987.'

Pahr insists that today's tourists have rising expectations so far as environment and heritage are concerned, and that demand is increasing for quality tourism products.

By the time I had finished Pahr, I had switched from the Circle Line to the Central Line and then to a No.15 bus and was reading Len Lickorish, a former director-general of the British Tourist Authority, who was explaining that while international tourism had expanded from 81 million arrivals in 1962 to 355 million in 1987, regional distribution has altered only slowly.

International travel is still concentrated heavily in just 20 countries, which account for two-thirds of international visitor movements. The US has lost share recently (from 25.5% to 21% in the five years to 1987); Europe has remained steady, and by 1987 the Middle East, Africa and South Asia still accounted for only 6.6% of world spend. In contrast, East Asia and the Pacific, ballooned from 5.2 to 12.3% of world spend between 1972 and 1987, and is now the fastest growing area in world travel.

Fig. C   From *The Financial Times* 1 April 1989

42 ASSESSMENT FOR SECTION TWO

Fig. A

Study Fig A.

1 Describe the scene in the photograph.

(5 marks)

2 What evidence is there of the cultural heritage of the place in the photograph?

(4 marks)

3 Describe the impact of tourism on a town you have studied.

(5 marks)

4 Read Fig B.

(a) Describe the attractions of a holiday in Kashmir.

(5 marks)

(b) Describe two ways in which the writer claims that tourism is damaging Kashmir.

(6 marks)

(c) What might be the views of one of the Kashmiri shopworkers in Srinagar about increasing tourism?

(4 marks)

(d) Study Fig C. Which of the two people do you agree with? Give the reasons for your choice.

(4 marks)

TOTAL: 33 marks

**THE GARDEN OF INDIA:
TOO LOVELY FOR ITS OWN GOOD**

(Adapted from an article by Paul Abrahams in *The Financial Times* 29.10.88)

Kashmir remains a place of beauty. The trouble is that, in the modern era, it has become too popular. Its beauty is threatened by tourists in great numbers who are overwhelming it. The reasons for its popularity are clear. Kashmir sits at the foot of the Himalayas, a land of lakes and houseboats, temples and ruins, birds and wild flowers. But a boat journey along the lakes and rivers of Kashmir demonstrates not only its charm, but also the damage that mass tourism is beginning to wreak.

The peaceful, rhythmic slapping of paddles in water was disturbed by the distant roar of a giant, floating combine harvester. Our boatmen explained that it was there to gather the weeds covering the lake. He said that Nagin Lake had not suffered from weeds until recently, but now the waste from 900-odd boats stationed around Srinagar provided perfect conditions for weed to grow. It was clogging the lakes and canals linking them, threatening both the lifestyle of the water-people who live by the river and the attraction of Kashmir itself.

As we approached Srinagar, the impact of mass tourism away from the lakes, on land, was also clear when we left the boat. The calm of the river was replaced by the bustle of the city. Ancient cars weaved along the roads, their drivers hooting continuously. We were confronted by a bewildering world of Campa-Cola, Kodachrome and craft shops with American Express stickers. Inside the stores the salesmen insisted on showing their papier-mache boxes covered with Moghul designs. We were ushered next door where we saw dark and exotic designs that claimed to be cheaper and better than any found in Harrods. Hurrying down to the boats, we fled from the commercialism. In the river a dead dog floated on its back.

Fig. B

As far as I'm concerned, the writer's criticisms are justified. I don't want to see Kashmir go the way of Thailand or Barbados. The traditional way of life of the people is threatened by mass tourism. It will change the country completely, replacing the ox-cart with the lorry, the paddle boat with the speed boat, the thatched hut with the brick house. I don't want to see just anyone coming to Kashmir on cheap package tours: Spain's the place for them.

A wealthy westerner who has visited Kashmir several times on holiday

Mass tourism offers the hope of an escape from the poverty which Kashmir has endured for so long. It may provide a paid job for landless labourers. It may fund an extension of electricity, water and road systems. Of course there is a threat to traditional Kashmiri culture, but a careful development policy will prevent this from occurring. The writer of the article just wants to keep Kashmir to himself and people like him, as some kind of living museum. Does he give a thought for the desires of the local people?

Kashmir Local Government official

Fig. C   Two views on the article *The Garden of India*

43 ASSESSMENT FOR SECTION THREE

0850 New Horizon Air Flight HZ201 from Malaga makes its final approach to Runway 15 at Birmingham International Airport. For the passengers on board, their holiday is almost over; for the crew of eight it is the end of another working day. For the aircraft, A310 Airbus G-ONHA, flight HZ200/1 Birmingham to Malaga and back to Birmingham, it is its first flight of the day with two more yet to do before tomorrow.

0900 G-ONHA halts at Stand 6. The aircraft doors are opened and the traffic agent boards, checks all is well and collects the aircraft's official paperwork. The hold doors are opened and the baggage handlers commence the off-load.

In the New Horizon Air Operations Centre the Captain and First Officer operating the aircraft's next flight, HZ154 to Faro, check their flight paperwork and the weather whilst their Cabin Crew near the end of their pre-flight briefing.

0905 Passengers start to disembark from the aircraft. The fuel bowser arrives. The caterers remove all the old stocks and replace with new. Meals and bars for both outbound and inbound flights are loaded at Birmingham. Toilet and fresh water requirements are serviced by the appropriate vehicles.

0910 The last of the passengers leave the airliner. Fuelling commences. The A310 will need over 10 000 litres. Cleaners board the aircraft and commence cleaning. The engineer checks the Technical Log for any defects. The inbound crew now disembark for Customs and de-briefing in the Crew Room.

0915 The cabin crew operating HZ154 to Faro arrive at the aircraft and commence their pre-flight checks – emergency and safety equipment, catering and toilets.

0920 Baggage off-load completed. Loading of the new baggage immediately commences.

0930 Cleaning completed. Cabin checked by Senior Crew Member. Captain and First Officer arrive and commence their pre-flight checks. The check-in desk inside the terminal building is closed. Final passenger and baggage figures are passed to New Horizon Air Operations.

0935 Message passed to Ground Hostess at Gate 6 that the aircraft is ready to receive passengers.

0940 Commence boarding passengers for flight HZ154. Fuelling completed. Catering completed and checked.

0945 Technical Log checked and signed by both Captain and Engineer.

0950 Baggage onload completed. Tug arrives to push the aircraft back. Loadsheet presented to Captain for checking and signing.

0955 Passenger boarding completed. Head count made by cabin crew. Hold doors are closed. All remaining Ground Staff disembark. Aircraft doors are closed.

1000 Airbridge removed from aircraft side. Captain requests start-up clearance from Air Traffic Control. Tug pushes G-ONHA from Stand 6.

At Faro, a similar process will take place and in 6 hours time G-ONHA will return to Birmingham for the final flight of the day, HZ622 to Corfu.

Fig. A   Turn-round

1 Study Fig A.
   (a) How long does the turn-round of the airliner take?

   (2 marks)

   (b) List ten types of job (other than the airliner's crew) which are involved in the turn-round of the airliner.

   (10 marks)

   (c) List the aircraft's flight schedule for the day.
   (3 marks)

   (d) Name the three countries which the aircraft visited that day.

   (3 marks)

   (e) How long before engine start-up do (i) the cabin crew (ii) the flight crew and (iii) the first passengers board the airliner?

   (3 marks)

   (f) How long does it take to fuel the airliner?
   (1 mark)

   (g) How long does it take to (i) off-load and (ii) on-load the baggage?

   (2 marks)

2 What is a curriculum vitae?

   (2 marks)

3 Name three things which you should do before attending an interview.

   (6 marks)

4 Write brief job descriptions for the following types of tourist-related employment:
   (a) Hotel receptionist

   (3 marks)

   (b) Hotel manager

   (3 marks)

   (c) Bar staff

   (2 marks)

5 Write a letter to an employer who has just provided you with a week's work experience at either (i) a travel agent or (ii) a hotel or (iii) a local country park. Describe the work which you did and state how useful you found the experience.

   (10 marks)

   TOTAL: 50 marks

INDEX